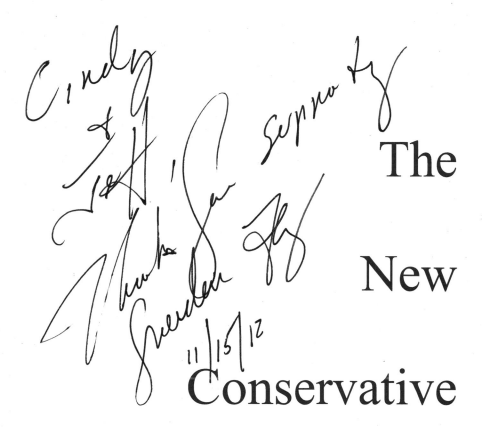

Cindy
+
Matt

Thanks for your support

Brendan De

11/15/12

The

New

Conservative

Paradigm

2ⁿᵈ Edition

Thomas G. Del Beccaro

ISBN: 978-0-578-08888-4

To my Mother for all of her courage and love

To my Father who introduced me to politics, and

To my daughter - everything I do, I do it for you

TABLE OF CONTENTS

Foreword
By Jack Cashill

It just so happened that after reading a draft of Tom Del Beccaro's *The New Conservative Paradigm*, I had a one-on-one meeting with a candidate for Congress. A sharp guy with a great reputation and good conservative instincts, this state legislator will have an excellent shot at unseating a five-term, Democratic incumbent.

What this candidate lacked, however, at least at this early stage of his campaign, was what the elder George Bush might have called "that vision thing."

Immediately after our meeting, I emailed him a draft of *The New Conservative Paradigm*. "Read this, please," I urged. As I explained, I have not seen anywhere a more lucid blueprint for helping America - in Ronald Reagan's words -to "begin again." My candidate read it and reacted as positively as I did.

The Roman poet Horace would have admired Del Beccaro's book as well. It is one of those rare political books that embodies his guiding aesthetic, *simplex munditiis*, or, in English, "elegant simplicity."

President Ronald Reagan embodied in person the aesthetic that Del Beccaro captures in print. As Del Beccaro makes clear, the political philosophy that guided Reagan was so streamlined by logic and so seasoned by experience that his opponents mistook its simple elegance for mere simplicity. History has proved them wrong and in spades.

Understandably, the spirit of President Reagan permeates the book, not just Reagan the ideologue, nor Reagan the optimist, but Reagan the leader.

The Democrats once had leaders. And Del Beccaro does not shy from giving John F. Kennedy credit where it is due. Like Reagan, Kennedy honored the three essentials of the new paradigm: pro-growth policies and reforms, specifically a belief in tax cuts; a belief in America and her defenses, and a respect for American traditions and values.

The Democrats lost their way during the presidency of Lyndon Johnson. While Johnson championed tax increases to "pay for" his wars on poverty and on Vietnamese Communists, his rebellious Democratic opposition championed poverty and the North Vietnamese. For a variety of reasons, none of them good. Democrats collectively abandoned their faith in America. They have not gotten it back.

As night follows day, the Democrats abandoned their faith in the American dream as well. Not since JFK have they had a national leader willing to actually lead and to inspire. Instead, they have settled for managers and not very competent ones at that. For both Jimmy Carter and Bill Clinton every issue had to be haggled over and every policy hacked out. There was no guiding logic to their plans and no respect shown for the intelligence of their constituents.

The 1432-page health care blueprint concocted by Hillary Clinton's 511-person secret task force in 1993 perfectly captured the condescension and clumsy incoherence of contemporary Democratic politics. Happily, the American people rejected stage management by the Clintons for what Del Beccaro nicely describes as "the theater of the possible."

Unfortunately, despite some shining moments, Republican leadership has all too often eschewed the possible for the seemingly safe. This strategy, alas, led to the loss of both houses of Congress in 2006, and Del Beccaro was not the least surprised.

What frustrates him and other Republicans as well is that the model for good leadership still resonates in our memory. What distinguishes Del Beccaro from those other Republicans is that he has converted that frustration into a lively, lucid prescription for positive and permanent change.

To make his case, Del Beccaro uses a deft mix of statistics, anecdotes, and historical data. His analysis is fresh, bright, and straightforward. There is nothing weary or wonkish about it. He reminds Republicans of just how simple and logical is the potential Republican path to success.

I just hope my candidate and a thousand others will follow it.

Introduction

Silent No More

**"To sin by silence when they should
protest makes cowards of men"
Ella Wilcox, American Poet**

In 2007, I asked the questions: Who will win the next presidential election? Which party will control Congress? Will it simply be the party that is ahead now? Or is there a winning paradigm for a successful political party regardless of which party is ahead now?

I wrote *The New Conservative Paradigm* in 2007 because History demonstrates that there is a winning paradigm and this *Second Edition* confirms that paradigm. Even so, since the first edition of this book much has changed.

Control of the House of Representatives has changed hands again – for the third time in 16 years after four decades of one-party rule. A presidency was decided and the Tea Party Movement began. *It seems the pace of change has changed as well.* It is fair to say, that in politics - as in life, there is little permanency. That applies to political books as well and so I thought it important to provide my readers with this 2nd edition of *The New Conservative Paradigm* inclusive of analyses of the 2008 and 2010 elections and a discussion of the Tea Party Movement.

~ ~ ~

The underlying theme of this book traces its start to 1980. It was then that Republicans began to reverse years of Congressional futility and began to move into the lead nationally. They did so because of the leadership of Ronald Reagan and his forging of a new political paradigm. It culminated with the election of George W. Bush in 2000 along with a Republican Congress. The Republicans' lead was apparent for all to see at that point. Just six years later, however, they abandoned a key part of ***The New Conservative Paradigm*** and visibly lost a good part of that lead in the 2006 Congressional elections and then altogether in 2008 by losing the Presidency.

It may not be entirely clear, for some, how the Republicans got ahead prior to 2006. Perhaps even less obvious is why, during 2005 and 2006, the Republican leaders chose to give up that lead or why the Democrats, in turn, forfeited much of their lead in 2010. As we approach the 2012 elections and the obvious fiscal problems in the decade ahead, Republicans simply must come to an understanding as to how Reagan once put Republicans ahead and how they can reclaim the presidency and Senate. As Reagan once said *without hesitation or doubt*:

"It can be done."

Given the stakes, nationally and internationally, it simply must be done – but it won't be done if we stand idly by. This book continues to set forth the optimistic formula as to how we can – a formula validated by the history of American politics from Eisenhower to today.

Back in 2007, I cautioned our leaders that leadership never stands still. True leadership continues to forge ahead - rather than being content with past victories. Leadership is also a bit like driving a race car. If you do it while looking over your shoulder too often, wondering if your competitor is closing ground - eventually you will crash. As we shall see in the pages ahead, the 2006 election was, in part, a lesson in the latter for Republicans.

With those thoughts about leadership in mind, I began writing the 1st Edition of this book amidst frustration. I literally started writing it, in early 2005, after watching *Meet the Press*. The late Tim Russert interviewed the majority and minority leaders in the US Senate at the time, Democrat Senator Richard Durbin of Illinois and Republican Mitch McConnell of Kentucky. Durbin was advocating more spending. No surprise so far. Then Russert asked him something to the effect of "how are you going to pay" for that spending? Durbin read right off the Left's talking points and claimed that, because of the "Bush tax cuts," the US government could not afford Durbin's proposed spending programs. Still no surprise.

What did Senator McConnell say about the tax cuts in response? What did the then Minority Leader in the Senate – a man with vast experience since the tax-cutting days of the Reagan Revolution - say in rebuttal to Durbin's attack on the Bush tax cuts? Did he continue to forge ahead as Reagan would? Sadly, no. Indeed, McConnell said nothing about the tax cuts. Absolutely nothing. He let Durbin get away with it. It was as if he thought Durbin was right. Worse yet, it was if McConnell had forgotten how Reagan put Republicans ahead.

Of course, Durbin was, and the Democrats still are, wrong. At the time the Bush tax cuts were enacted, the Nation was in a "Clinton-tax-increase-induced-9/11-exacerbated" recession –

and, this just in Senator McConnell, recessions cause tax revenues to drop. On the flip side, after the Bush tax cuts were fully enacted in 2003, the US economy reversed its downward trend, roared back to life - and so did revenues: a 5% increase in 2004, a 15% increase in 2005, a similar increase in 2006 and a large increase in 2007. Yearly revenues grew by over $700 billion in the wake of those tax cuts before other government policies hurt the economy. Those increases were not unlike the revenue booms that occurred after the Reagan tax cuts, the Kennedy/Johnson tax cuts, the Coolidge tax cuts and the many other examples in history when moribund economies were jumped-started with tax cuts.

Those economic facts remain true to this day. As Republicans, Senator Mitch McConnell included, we need to be more than just aware of that history. It needs to be a part of our vision; we need a strategy for its continued implementation and we must have the ability to articulate it when necessary.

In large part, and in an effort to be *Silent No More*, that is why I wrote *The New Conservative Paradigm,* and founded Politicalvanguard.com – a conservative e-magazine. It is also why I would go on to become the Republican Party Chairman of California.

~ ~ ~

As for what has changed, in the 1st Edition of this book I noted that years ago, in the era when Democrats began "Blaming America First," Richard Nixon referred to many voters and volunteers who disagreed with that sentiment as the **Silent Majority** of American politics. He insisted that that the "Silent Majority" supported his efforts over those of the dissident Democrats.

I noted that by 2007, for many of us, we were **Silent No More**. Almost innocently by comparison to now, I mentioned that:

> "the frustrated and more fill the airways with talk radio calls, we write letters to the editor and otherwise volunteer in ever larger numbers. We remember how Reagan broke our silence and how he boldly affirmed his beliefs and changed us, a Nation and a World. We recognize that Reagan's greatest investment was in the American Spirit - our Spirit - not government - and we do not quite understand why the current crop of leaders will not live up to his calling. Others wonder if our current leaders truly understand the Reagan Revolution."

Little did I know that that frustration would reach a boiling point when the newly-elected President Obama pushed through, without a single Republican vote, an unprecedented spending bill that was dubbed economic "stimulus" at the same time he offered Americans a $75 billion fund to pay for Americans' delinquent mortgages. That combination proved to be political kerosene which exploded when TV reporter Rick Santelli called for a *Tea Party*. Since then, President Obama picked several more huge fights with the American people, including on Cap & Trade and ObamaCare, and the Tea Party became a nearly irresistible force.

~ ~ ~

Returning to 1980, in rather simple terms, Reagan started a political realignment – a reversal of political fortunes – that lasted for more than two decades. Reagan did so not by wanting to *manage* government. Instead, Reagan was an inspirational *leader* of **We the People** who *changed the course* of government.

Reagan did all of the above by championing what I call the Three Pillars of ***The New Conservative Paradigm***:

(1) Pro-Growth policies/reforms,

(2) Belief in America and her defense, and

(3) Respect for American traditions and values.

This book will chronicle that reversal of fortunes of each major party in recent years. It will also highlight Reagan's political and economic success, based on policies that empowered **We the People**. I will contrast that with the presidents that sought to manage societal change through social programs and who, not coincidentally, enjoyed far less success.

The New Conservative Paradigm also will feature its first messenger, Democrat John F. Kennedy, along with others that laid the groundwork for *The New Conservative Paradigm* and still others who strengthen *The New Conservative Paradigm*.

Finally, this book will also explore how the Republican Party can turn the Democrat losses of 2010 into Republican momentum in time for 2012 and how it can then stay ahead in the difficult decade ahead. At the time I finished the 1st Edition of this book in 2007, the severe problems of our explosive growth in government had yet to arrive. They are here now. They have arrived for our Country as a whole and in many states, counties and cities as well.

If you are yet unconvinced that government growth is a problem, you need only to look at this Heritage Foundation chart to catch a glimpse of the unsustainable growth of our federal government measured in 2010 dollars.

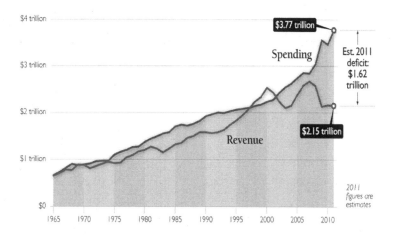

Federal spending, adjusted for inflation, is more than 6 times the size it was in 1965 and it has nearly doubled in the last decade. Most of that growth in spending has gone towards social welfare programs. Yet the percentage of Americans in poverty, as measured by the government, remains nearly identical today as it was in 1965 – around 14%. In other words, we have spent well over $13 trillion dollars "fighting" poverty – with current spending over $1 trillion per year - with virtually no return on investment.

In 2007, prior to the Obama presidency, I wrote that "We have no choice but to confront that growth." To date we have not - and now we have yearly *deficits* larger than the entire budgets of the 1980s and more than double the budgets of the 1960's (adjusted for inflation). The federal government's debt has moved to the top of voters' concerns and, in 2011, just 9% of us believe we will see a balanced federal budget in their lifetime.

However ominous that sentiment, one thing we can say is that when it comes to the American politics, ***Something Has Changed***.

Chapter 1

Something Has Changed

"Things do not change; *we change*."
Henry David Thoreau

Things have certainly changed – indeed many things have changed. The Democrats of Zell Miller's[1] fond memories were once the party of tax cuts. Those tax cuts are now the domain of the Republicans. From Franklin Roosevelt's "Arsenal of Democracy,"[2] the Democrats morphed into the party of

---

[1] During the 2004 presidential campaign, Democrat Senator from Georgia Zell Miller became a National figure when he endorsed Republican George Bush for President over Democrat John Kerry. Miller also supported the Bush tax policies and gave a stirring speech at the 2004 Republican National Convention.

[2] In the midst of World War II, Franklin Roosevelt referred to Detroit's auto industry as the "Arsenal of Democracy" because it converted to war material production. The phrase was actually coined by a French businessman Jean Monnet – who used the phrase in a meeting with advisors of Roosevelt.

disarmament and retreat - and with that transition - the Republicans became the party most trusted with national defense.

Before that, and for almost 40 years, from the late 1950s to the mid-1990s, Congress was the playground of the Democrats who held perennial majorities. At their height, in 1965, the Democrats had the White House, a 295 - 140 majority in the House of Representatives and a 68 - 32 majority in the US Senate.

From 1994 to 2006, by contrast, the Republican Party held sway in the halls of Congress. Further:

- by 2008, in 27 of the last 39 years, the Republicans held the White House

- 97 of the 100 fastest growing counties in the Country voted for President Bush in 2004

- In 2004, President George W. Bush became the first president in 16 years to get more than 50% of the vote.

- President George W. Bush was the first president to increase his party's representation in both Houses of Congress in three consecutive elections in over 50 years.
- The Republican Party enjoyed over a decade of Congressional dominance in the House and Senate between 1994 and 2006.

Thereafter, he was asked not to use it again and it became the subject of one of Roosevelt's famous "fireside chats."

- In 2004, a majority of the US Governorships were held by Republicans.

- In 2004, the Republicans, for the first time in history, held the Governorships of the 4 largest states in the Country: California, New York, Florida and Texas.

Then, in a matter of 3 years, between 2005 and 2008, those trends appeared to reverse and then reverse again in 2010.

Did *things* change during those times? Or did *we* change? Regardless of whether you agree with Thoreau - we are in a different age.

Where once an icon from our past told us "that's the way it is,"[3] unlikely media comets such as Dennis Miller tell us the way it should be. Cable's Fox News lays claim to being *Fair and Balanced*, swamps CNN and MSNBC in the ratings regularly and even the networks on important stories such as political convention coverage.

For pure attitude and energy, Ann Coulter makes the cover of *Time* Magazine, while Michelle Malkin and Laura Ingraham, among others, hold the higher ground against the likes of whomever the Left puts up. Even in California, Conservative talk radio - featuring the bombastic in the form of KFI's John and Ken in Los Angeles to the more straightforward Dennis Prager and Hugh Hewitt as well as Brian Sussman of KSFO in

---

[3] CBS' Walter Cronkite, once dubbed the most trusted man in America, signed off each night by reciting that phrase.

San Francisco - rules the airwaves while Air America, the liberals attempt at a talk radio network, wallowed in bankruptcy before dropping off the air. Meanwhile, the Internet and its bloggers run roughshod over the *New York Times* and the *Boston Globe* – not to mention CBS.[4]

The question remains, however, exactly what changed and how did it change? Did Republicans come up with better candidates for a period of time? More likable candidates? Better policies? The National Security Age/Homeland Security Age? Social issues? Economic Issues? Did they lose because of those things in 2006 and 2008 only to regain them in 2010? Or is it all simply the turn of the wheel - each Party's moment in the sun?

Simply stated, there was a change – even if the 2005/2006 Congressional Republicans failed to notice the change - and any analysis of that change starts with President Ronald Reagan.

~   ~   ~

Years before the Reagan presidency, during the early 1960s, the Democrats were in the lead and enjoyed huge

---

[4] In the weeks before the 2004 election, CBS' and Dan Rather's hit piece regarding President Bush's military service was debunked by diligent bloggers.

majorities in Congress – majorities built in part on the tax cutting/pro-freedom ideas of John F. Kennedy.   The Republicans, for their part, were the contrary party or the Party that said *No* -   No to the Kennedy tax cuts (that's not a misprint) and no to the *Great Society* excesses of the Democrats as the decade wore on.   It was a most unenviable position for the Republicans because the Democrats were buying votes with *Great Society* programs and earning votes with the Kennedy/Johnson tax cuts. The Republicans, on the other hand, did not have a positive message of their own, just a *contrary* message.

During the late 1960s and 1970s, the Democrats revived their New Deal role as the *Tax & Spend* Party and the Republicans became the "Tax and Spend-a-Little-Less Party." That still meant, however, that the Republicans were not really offering something – they were offering something *less*.   All told, those "something less" messages earned the Republicans a solid *minority* position in Congress.

Enter Ronald Reagan – stage *right* or, as we shall come to find, from the theatre of the possible. From the ash heap of our national malaise under Jimmy Carter, arose candidate and then President Ronald Reagan.

Reagan was a champion of true hope. At his core, Reagan believed in empowering people *not* government. Amidst the struggles of the 1970s, Reagan well understood that our Nation would succeed not by falling back on more government intervention but by creating the conditions by which individuals, families and the American Spirit could move ahead.

Consistent with those beliefs, as president, Reagan sided with **We the People** over government. He enacted large, supply-side, personal income tax cuts and tax cuts for employers. Those tax cuts restored freedom to overburdened Americans – and in granting that freedom, Reagan energized a Nation. Not satisfied with that alone, Reagan sought to preserve freedom by championing government reform and he restricted the growth of government on whose leave freedom depends.

It was a *positive* agenda and his pro-growth/reform policies not only created an economic boom and cured America of its malaise, but they also restored America's sense of purpose and its pride. Simply stated, President Reagan became the national, if not world, purveyor of America's unique brand of **Optimism** – joining other great leaders of *History* who well understood that such a positive disposition is the father of political inspiration. All of that was a winning formula because America, from the Mayflower to Microsoft, has been about **Optimism**.

Reagan changed the dynamics of presidential politics as well. Since Reagan:

- All presidential candidates have been, and are now, defined by whether they are pro-growth or pro-government – or quite simply by their stance on taxes – the new fault-line of American politics.

- The *No New Tax Pledge* took hold.

- Presidential candidates either were for cutting taxes or suffered the consequences.

- The Republicans became the Majority Party in Congress – until they squandered that lead away in 2006 only regain it in 2010.

That reformation of the national debate and of the national character was among the many changes *History* owes to Reagan. President George W. Bush, in no uncertain terms, at the outset of his presidency embraced the policies and politics of optimism, tax cuts, freedom and the belief that we can achieve more.

For their part, during the Bush presidency, the leadership of the Democrats appeared not to be for anything – instead, they were *against* most everything: wars for freedom, tax cuts, social security reform,[5] and government reform in general, as they are again today in the second year of Obama's presidency. So pure was their opposition mentality that despite the passage of months and months after the president announced their 2005 reforms - the Democrats did not announce a single, meaningful

---

[5] The president sought reform of the obviously troubled Social Security system in early 2005.

counter-proposal. In the 2006 Congressional elections, the Democrats did not campaign with a platform and offered no positive agenda. Instead, they offered opposition to President Bush and the Iraq War and relied on the discontent of conservative and Independent voters to win.

Once in power, in 2007, the Congressional Democrats accomplished little of note – a by-product of their empty, negative campaign that produced no mandate for a specific change – and, in doing so, House Leader Nancy Pelosi's Democrats presided over Congressional approval ratings of historic lows. As such, it is fair to say that the Democrats, under the George W. Bush presidency, were the party of criticism not suggestion – the *Party of No*. Once Obama got into office, the Democrats returned to their tax and spend ways with unprecedented fervor – even for them – and blocked true reform after they lost Congress in the Fall of 2010.

In the final analysis, the Democrat leadership, nationally and in many states, does not embrace ***Optimism*** nor true reform, nor lower taxes. To the contrary, the philosophy of the Democrat leadership can be distilled into this simple paradigm:

If you make it - they will take it
- and if you don't have it -
they have a program for it.

In other words, their philosophy is to punish those who succeed and to promote dependency. They believe not in self-reliance, but in government programs. Indeed, it would appear that they prefer that the government safety net become a hammock – all of which amounts to nothing more than a throwback to the days of buying votes with government handouts. It is a negative agenda filled with yesterday's ideas and an agenda that was badly losing in the battle for the hearts and minds of American voters – until the Republican leaders forgot the lessons of the Reagan Revolution and lost their way in the years leading up to the 2006 election.

In the coming pages, we will focus on the changes fostered by the *Reagan Revolution*. Those changes, however, are not the end of our analysis, but instead, the beginning. It is so, because policies of empowering Americana, i.e. pro-growth policies, although the dominant governing policy, were not the only governing themes of Ronald Reagan.

President Reagan also managed a reversal of fortunes between the two parties on the issue of who is fighting for our families and their traditions. He also solidified the Republicans' lead as protectors of the American homeland. In doing all of that, and by transforming the national debate and the national character, Reagan established a *New Conservative Paradigm* and inspired *New Conservatives*.

In order to really appreciate the *Reagan Revolution*, however, it will be important to truly understand more than just the changes Reagan set in motion. We must understand his part - in light of the whole – and we especially must understand what came before Reagan: the Soul of a "Me Too" Party – so that Republicans never become so again.

Chapter 2

The Soul of a "Me Too" Party

"Mondale has the soul of a vice president."
Sen. Eugene McCarthy 1976

Long before "powerful" vice presidents such as Dick Cheney or Al Gore, vice presidents were to be seen, not heard. They had a political soul – too often vacant. Minority parties, at times, have had that vacant soul as well. It is important to note that they don't just wake up one day as the Minority Party – they get to be that the old-fashioned way – *they earn it*. And so it was for the Republican Party, lackluster for more than two decades - from the late fifties through the sixties and into the late seventies.

The Numbers Don't Lie

In 1953, Republican Gen. Dwight D. Eisenhower was president. The Republicans controlled the House of Representatives and the US Senate. In the House, Republicans outnumbered Democrats 221 to 213 with one Independent. The Republicans held a slim majority in the Senate, 48 – 46 with 2 Independents.

It would be 42 years before Republicans would again lay claim to that majority status in the House.

In between:

- No less than three times, or for six years, the Democrats would have more than *twice* as many House Members as the Republicans (1965: 295 - 140), (1975: 291 – 144), (1977: 292 – 143)

- Seven times, or for a total of fourteen years, the Democrats had at least *100* more members in the House than the Republicans: (1959, 1965, 1975, 1977, 1979, 1983, 1991)[6]

The Republicans faired not much better in the US Senate. After the 1954 election, the Democrats held a slim one seat advantage, 48 – 47, (with one Independent) in the Senate. In the aftermath of the 1957/58 Eisenhower recession, that

---

[6] Compare that to 2005's "slim" 30 seat Republican House majority which many viewed as a significant margin.

advantage became wide and deep – jumping to a 64 to 34 advantage after the 1958 election.   Six times thereafter, the Democrats sat more than 60 US Senators in the US Congress - reaching a high of 68 Senate Seats after the 1964 election.

It's rather hard to argue with those numbers or their message: The Republicans were the Minority Party in Congress for years upon years after "controlling" the White House, the House of Representatives and the Senate in 1953.

The only question is why.   Fortunately, the answer is plain enough, at least to the *New Conservatives*.

The Road to Minority*hood*
"Affordable Tax Cuts" – The Eisenhower Years

To say that the Republicans controlled the White House in 1953 is factually correct but perhaps overstated in effect. *Republican* Dwight Eisenhower was not a staunch Republican by any modern standards.

Indeed, four years before he accepted the Republican nomination, two Democrats, Claude Pepper and James Roosevelt, attempted to woo Eisenhower to run for the 1948 *Democratic* nomination.   Eisenhower, however, did not accept their overtures.   Instead, Eisenhower decided to seek, and ultimately win the Republican nomination in 1952.

Obviously, history hardly indicates that Eisenhower was philosophically   well-defined.   Could   you   imagine   the

Democrats asking Reagan to be their nominee in 1980? No, Eisenhower was a popular war hero. He was the former Supreme Allied Commander in Europe and Commander of NATO and, understandably, his presidency was dominated by managing foreign affairs.

Perhaps because he believed that post-World War II Americans were weary, or because he lacked the vision to do so, Eisenhower's domestic agenda was devoid of any attempt to challenge the American people to achieve new domestic heights. It was not like Washington's that forged a Nation, nor Monroe's that settled much of the known West, nor Jackson's that broadened our democracy, nor Lincoln's presidency that saved a Nation. It also was not like that the Presidencies of Harding and Coolidge who restarted the American economy that was weighed down by exorbitant tax rates in wake of World War I.

Simply stated, Eisenhower was not a doctrinaire politician committed to an agenda and that was all too clear when it came to American prosperity and taxes. Despite a landslide victory for Republicans in 1952, in what would become a familiar signpost along the *Road to Minorityhood* for Republicans, Eisenhower remained politically and economically cautious. On the issue of taxes, Eisenhower early on would declare:

"We cannot ***afford*** to reduce taxes, reduce income until we have in sight a program of expenditure that shows that the factors of income and outgo will be balanced."

In Eisenhower's 1954 State of the Union, he again made his aversion to tax cuts very clear. Eisenhower stated:

"Six days ago individual income taxes were reduced and the excess profits tax expired . . . These tax reductions are justified <u>only</u> because of the substantial reductions we already have made and are making in governmental expenditures. As additional reductions in expenditures are brought gradually but surely into sight, further reductions in taxes can and will be made . . . When budget savings and sound governmental financing are assured, tax burdens should be reduced so that taxpayers may spend their own money in their own way."

His commitment to tax cuts was muddled but his message quite clear: tax cuts would *only* be justifiable if the ***government*** could ***afford*** to cut them, i.e. if the government hadn't otherwise spent the money – only then may taxpayers keep and spend their own money. It was a two-part equation and ***government spending was paramount over private initiative***. It was a policy that sided with the management of government over the inspirational needs of ***We the People***.

Beyond that, tax relief seemingly was not an instrument of economic policy - let alone a powerful means for generating growth. Instead, it was to be tolerated politically if spending was controlled.

Perhaps what is most remarkable, to readers of today, about Eisenhower's statement in his 1954 State of the Union address is: (1) that it was made in the midst of a recession and (2) the top personal income tax rate was 91% at the time. Faced with such a suffocating tax rate, between July 1953 and May 1954, there was a 2.7% *decline* in real US GDP. Eisenhower was obviously unmoved by the recession and instead was primarily focused on balancing the federal budget during the economic downturn.

Eisenhower's reluctance to cut taxes during a recession, however economically wrong, was not unheard of at the time. To the contrary, Republican President Hoover, in 1930, well after the stock market crash of October 1929, and amidst a bad recession, raised the top personal tax rate from 25% to 63%. That tax increase helped foster the Great Depression, caused federal revenues to decline and set Republicans back politically for years to come. Why would Hoover take such drastically wrong action? Why would Hoover choose the concerns of government over the needs of the American people during a bad recession? Because he too mistakenly believed that raising tax rates, as opposed to fostering economic growth, was the path to increasing revenues and balancing the federal budget. For his part, Democrat FDR continued that misguided policy and later raised the top rate to 79% - an act that prolonged the Great Depression.

Returning our attention to Eisenhower, what was less remarkable, or perhaps more predictable, was that Eisenhower faced a second, more severe, recession just three years later in 1958. That Fall, the Democrats gained 15 seats in the US Senate. That election made it clear that the war hero was not an economic hero. Less than two years later, a third recession hit and the US was ready for a change away from a cautious manager of government in favor of a vibrant leader of *We the People*.

The Road to Minorityhood Continues with . . .
A Contrast in All Respects

President Eisenhower was, by all measures, cautious. His leadership style has been variously described as "oblique"[7] and "easy going." "He took his party to the center of the road, 'where the traction is best and where you can bring the most people along with you.'" His critics saw his "Middle Way" as one without the vision or courage to engage the important

---

[7] *The Hidden-Hand Presidency: Eisenhower as Leader* by Fred I. Greenstein

social issues of the day."[8] The election of JFK, in the Fall of 1960, would change all that.

Whether you were a fan or not of the new president, the contrast between Eisenhower the *manager* and John F. Kennedy the *leader* could not be more pronounced *and not only in style.* – Kennedy was not interested in managing government – he wanted to challenge the American people.

Kennedy confronted the stagnant economic times of the late 1950s by asking Americans, in his campaign, to confront the "New Frontier." He faced a tax system that, in 1962, required the top one percent to pay a whopping 20 percent of all income taxes. The top marginal rate was still that incredible 91% - meaning that for every additional dollar that a taxpayer in the top tax bracket made, 91¢ of it went to the federal government.

Boldly, President Kennedy set a course 180° away from his predecessor on the issue of taxes. From the article "Sorry Ted: JFK cut taxes" by W. James Antle III, we read:

> "Kennedy call[ed] for 'an across-the-board, top-to-bottom cut in personal and corporate income taxes.' He argued 'that our present tax system ... exerts too heavy a drag on growth ... siphons out of the private economy too large a share of personal and business purchasing

---

[8] "Dwight Eisenhower, The Cautious Warrior,"
http://www.historywise.com/KoTrain/COurses/DE/DE_Domestic_Affairs.ht
m

power, [and] reduces the financial incentives for personal effort, investment, and risk-taking.

Kennedy explicitly endorsed rate reductions for high-income taxpayers in language that foreshadowed supply-side economics, proposing tax cuts '**for those in the middle and upper brackets, who can thereby be encouraged to undertake additional efforts and... invest more capital.**'[9]

In his January 24, 1963 message to Congress, Kennedy completed the revolution in thought by stating:

"I repeat: our practical choice is not between a tax-cut deficit and budgetary surplus. It is between two kinds of deficits: a chronic deficit of inertia, as the unwanted result of inadequate revenues and a restricted economy; or a temporary deficit of transition, resulting from a **tax cut designed to boost the economy, increase tax revenues**, and achieve--and I believe this can be done--a budget surplus."

Just weeks before that, Kennedy declared his pro-growth, supply-side *Optimistic* beliefs in earnest by stating:

"It is a paradoxical truth that tax rates are too high today and tax revenues are too low and the soundest way to raise the revenues *in the long run* is to cut tax rates now."[10]

---

[9] http://www.enterstageright.com/archive/articles/0301jfk.htm

[10] Kennedy's speech to the Economic Club of New York, December 14, 1962

As you read those words, it is more than apparent that Kennedy would be no Eisenhower. Gone was any notion that tax cuts were a political luxury to be *afforded* only if government spending was under control. Gone was any discussion of spending at all. The issue was no longer a two-part equation. Replacing such intellectual inertia was the prospect of "a temporary deficit of transition," the result of a tax cut designed to "*increase* tax revenues." **Taxes became a one-part equation – an economic policy instrument for growth**.

In his gallant style and with sheer ***Optimism***, Kennedy sided with ***We the People*** over government and declared that ***tax cuts not tax increases*** were the way to balance the budget – the complete opposite of Republican Hoover, Democrat Roosevelt, Democrat Truman and Republican Eisenhower. How would tax cuts do that? They would do so by restoring freedom to Americans and by inspiring and fostering economic growth in the private sector not government programs. It was Reagan*esque* before Reagan. Indeed, it was Kennedy*esque* – and along with his strong defense of America and its ideals warrants recognizing JFK as ***The First New Conservative***. It was also more than just an economic policy. The transition from Eisenhower to Kennedy was a dynamic change in philosophy and momentum.

Indeed, the tax cuts were but one small aspect of the ***Optimistic***, can-do aspect of Kennedy's brief tenure. On the issue of world peace, Kennedy proclaimed he was seeking a broader achievement:

> "What kind of peace do I mean? What kind of peace do we seek? Not a Pax Americana enforced on the world by American weapons of war. Not the peace of the grave or the security of the slave . . . I am talking about genuine peace, the kind of peace that makes life on earth worth living, the kind that enables men and nations to grow and to hope and to build a better life for their children -- not merely peace for Americans but peace for all men and women -- not merely peace in our time, but peace in all time."

Kennedy renewed the call for the US to land a man on the moon – not someday, but he challenged America to achieve it *before the decade was out.* He founded the Peace Corps and boldly claimed in the face of the Soviet Union: "All free men, wherever they may live, are citizens of Berlin, and, therefore, as a free man, I take pride in the words 'Ich bin ein Berliner.'"

In those and other respects, *Kennedy's Camelot* was not synonymous with *Eisenhower's Caution.* The leader of the Democrats was young, ambitious and ***Optimistic*** – and he had an economic policy to match it – tax cuts that could "achieve" growth - again, not by relying on government but individual initiative.

History, or more specifically, his assassination, did not allow Kennedy to see his agenda enacted and, in the long run, that would result in the Democrats becoming a Minority Party. In the short run, and in an odd historical twist, his *Optimistic* agenda was adopted by a vice president turned president who hardly represented Camelot.

~   ~   ~

President Lyndon Johnson was no John Kennedy. He was older, much less charismatic, and embodied little of Kennedy's gallant style. Nevertheless, Johnson sought the enactment of Kennedy's agenda. At the outset of his 1964 State of the Union, Johnson declared:

> "Let us carry forward the plans and programs of John Fitzgerald Kennedy -- not because of our sorrow or sympathy, but because *they are right*.

On the issue of tax cuts, Johnson posited that:

> [E]very individual American taxpayer and every corporate taxpayer will benefit from the earliest possible passage of the pending tax bill from both the new investment it will bring and the new jobs that it will create."

By making that statement, Johnson appeared to accept and understand the pro-growth nature of the proposed tax cut – but did he really think that Kennedy's programs were right? The answer, as the unfolding years would demonstrate, was no.

Indeed, by his very next statement in that 1964 State of the Union, any understanding or commitment to pro-growth tax policies was belied – a statement which demonstrated that the Democrats had lost their **Optimistic** leader and replaced him with someone more managerial and economically cautious, someone more like Eisenhower. Indeed, the seeds of a future Reversal of Party Fortunes were sown when Johnson went on to say:

"That tax bill has been thoroughly discussed for a year. Now we need action. **The new budget clearly allows it.**"

Such a statement was reflective of a long-time tax and spend legislator and *Eisenhower could not have said it much better – tax cuts were acceptable because the government could afford them*. Combined with he Great Society programs, once again, *We the People* were not be challenged to succeed. Instead, we were offered cradle to grave assistance. Johnson would go on to subordinate our needs to the needs of government and once again we had a president more interested in government action than individual freedom.

To Be Contrary or to Be Right?

At the time of Johnson's State of the Union request for a tax cut in 1964, the Republicans had a clear choice: whether to be *right* or whether to be *contrary*. Given Johnson's ambiguous message on tax cuts, it would have been possible to grab the **Optimistic** mantle of pro-growth leadership away from Johnson and the Democrats and to come down on the side of individuals and families. The Republican leadership, however, chose to be largely *contrary*.

In fact, Republicans in significant numbers opposed the Kennedy/Johnson tax cuts – including Barry Goldwater who called the cuts "gimmickry" during the 1964 presidential campaign. Later in the campaign, in a reversal, Goldwater proposed his own set of tax cuts. His characterization of the Kennedy cuts as "gimmickry," however, made it impossible for Republicans to get out in front of the issue and many wound up opposing the Kennedy/Johnson cuts. Obviously, that left the voters without a clear message of whether the Republicans understood the purpose or value of tax cuts.[11]

---

[11] To some degree, perhaps, the Republicans of the early 1960s can be forgiven in their opposition to tax cuts. American economic history was not as clear as it was by 1967. As we shall see, the Republicans would have no such excuse by 1967 and certainly not today.

Time proved that to be contrary and/or ambivalent was to be wrong and Kennedy to be right. Over the next three years, the Kennedy/Johnson tax cuts produced average, annual growth rates in excess of 6% from 1964 to 1967. Combined with Johnson's Great Society, the Democrats got the credit for the tax cuts and appeared to have cornered the national political market: tax cuts for those paying taxes, including individuals and business owners, and social programs for the middle and lower economic classes.

Committed to Minorityhood,
The Republican Party of "Me Too" Emerges

In 1965, the Kennedy/Johnson Democrats enjoyed huge majorities in Congress: a 295 to 140 margin in the House and a 68 to 32 majority in the Senate. Faced with the popular (and effective) tax cuts, as well as new spending programs, for their part, the Republicans developed a message deficit – they were at first the "Party of No." Many opposed the Kennedy/Johnson tax cuts on the grounds of "fiscal responsibility." Most opposed the spending increases of the Great Society on the same grounds. But that left them with very little to offer voters, no positive message of their own – just a *contrary* message.

How did the Republicans handle that message deficit as the decade wore on? What would they do in the wake of Johnson's decision not to run a second time and Nixon's victory? They simply failed to seize the opening. In some respects, the Republican Party chose to dig an even deeper hole even though large political opportunities presented themselves.

The first such opportunity came in 1967. Consistent with his Eisenhower-like wariness of tax cuts, and notwithstanding the success of the Kennedy tax cut programs, starting in 1967, President Johnson pursued a tax *increase* which was signed into law in 1968. It purportedly was needed "pay" for the Vietnam War and the Democrats' Great Society spending.

In other words, and rather incredibly, despite the 62% increase in federal revenues kicked off by the tax cuts and generated by an economy growing on average 6% or more a year, President Johnson and the Democrats unilaterally disarmed themselves on the issue of tax cuts. They had resumed their *New Deal* tax and spend ways and newly titled them as the *War on Poverty* and the *Great Society*.[12] Again, it was clear that the Democrats no longer had an **Optimistic** pro-growth leader of **We the People** but instead a proponent of social change through government.

At that moment, in the race for political leadership, the Republicans clearly were behind the Democrats in Congress

---

[12] In his 1964 State of the Union speech, Johnson dubbed his request for social welfare spending a "War on Poverty." Those programs were part of Johnson's Great Society – a series of federal programs promoted by the Democrats to eliminate poverty and racial injustice.

and among voters as far as party affiliation.   Logically, therefore, in order to overtake the Democrats, the Republicans running for Congress would need to offer voters something other than what the Democrats were offering – otherwise voters would not have compelling reason to vote the Congressional Democrats out. The Republicans needed to offer better policies at the same time they exposed the weakness of the Democrats' policies.   In that way, defeating an incumbent party is no different than defeating a single incumbent politician.

It is within that context that the clear tax cut opening began to emerge for the Republicans.   The Republicans, however, failed to seize that opening.

It did not have to be so.   By 1967, the lessons of the Kennedy cuts were plain to see. The economy was performing brilliantly and tax revenues were on the rise. That experience could be matched with the lessons of the tax cuts of the early 1920s. Back then, **Republicans** Warren G. Harding and Calvin Coolidge cut the top personal income rate from 71% to 24%. The economy responded and grew 59%, a phenomenon dubbed *The Roaring 20s.*

Armed with that knowledge, the Republicans of the mid 1960s still did not become the party of tax cuts.   To the contrary, they would become the "Me Too" Party.

Indeed, history recorded that in 1967, the Republicans did not make a name for themselves through opposition to the Johnson tax increase.   In 1969, despite winning the White

House with President Nixon, the Republicans would do no better. Nixon responded to what was becoming a growing economic inflationary crisis by adopting the position of the *Democrats* at the time. Nixon and the Democrat led Congress sided with government over **We the People** and *increased* taxes by doubling the capital gains rate – as anti-growth a tax measure as you can dream up – all in a renewed effort to pay for government – ***not by cutting taxes but by raising tax rates***.

Lacking his own vision to inspire Americans to achieve domestically, Nixon would cement his role as a champion of government "solutions" by pulling nearly every lever of government he could to address the growing economic problems. Nixon's efforts included imposing wage and price controls. But that was not all. On the spending side, under Nixon and the Democrat Congress, "entitlement spending grew from 6.5 percent of GDP in 1969 to 10.6 percent in 1975, an unprecedented increase."[13]

With that combination, Congressional Republicans, led by President Nixon, chose the worst of all political worlds – behind the Democrats in the race for Congress and offering the voters virtually the same domestic policies - they truly had become the "Me Too" Party. They too were the party of tax

---

[13] "Do These Deficits Look Familiar?" by Jonathan Rauch
http://www.reason.com/rauch/012604.shtml

increases, government and higher spending – and to no real political avail.   Two years after Nixon's 1968 victory, in the 1970 Congressional election, the Democrats still won 255 House seats, the Republicans 180 – all because they offered the voters no meaningful alternative to the Democrats.

In 1972, Nixon won in a landslide: 61% to 38% in the popular vote and 520 – 17 in the Electoral College.   Despite that historically successful presidential election, however, the gap between Democrats and the Democrat–lite-Republicans closed to only 242 Democrats and 192 Republicans in Congress - and that narrowing proved short-lived.   In the aftermath of Watergate,[14] the margin ballooned again, in 1974, to 291 Democrats and 144 Republicans.

Thus, by the early 1970s, and despite two presidential victories, the Republicans emerged as largely the same as the Democrats – a "Me Too" Party on spending and a party that supported anti-growth tax policies. Worse yet, Republicans had by in large become proponents of government not **We the People**. Such lesser policies and lack of leadership would not and did not change the political dynamic of the time. The Republicans would remain a distinctly Minority Party.

---

[14] Nixon resigned on August 8, 1974.

The Ford Presidency Provides
Little More Inspiration to Voters

President Gerald Ford inherited not only the office of the presidency but also the tax-increasing, high spending policies of Presidents Johnson and Nixon. Those policies failed America and left the Country with a growing economic crisis. The catch phrase for that crisis was something called "stagflation." It referred to the prevailing economic condition of the time: low economic growth rates, rising consumer prices and a weak labor market. Normally, lower growth rates tend to lead to a softening of prices. However, during this period of time, inflation surged – due in large part to poor government monetary policy that caused increases in the Consumer Price Index.

What did President Ford due in response? Ford too would manage government. He fought Democrats on spending and had government provide a $50 dollar rebate for taxpayers – yet another non-pro-growth tax bill given that it provided no future economic incentives. Instead, it was a "reward" and a paltry one at that, for a prior years' activity. The economy, for its part, did not respond as Ford hoped. Inflation remained historically high, despite his Whip Inflation Now policies featuring "WIN" buttons, and the growth continued to be anemic.

In the November presidential election of 1976, President Ford lost to a peanut farmer from Georgia, Jimmy Carter. It is, of course, conventional wisdom that Ford lost that election because of his pardon of Richard Nixon in the wake of Watergate. Surely, Watergate and the ensuing pardon hobbled Ford and the Republicans heading into the 1976 election. Despite that, Ford nearly caught Carter at the end.

Given that, was Watergate and the pardon really the only reason Ford lost, or was it something else in addition to that? In truth, there was something else: the very bad economic condition that the tax increasing, big spending Nixon laid at Ford's feet. It was a storyline that Ford did little to turn around. As they went to the polls, voters well noticed that poor economic condition of the Country over the previous two years which included unemployment as high as 9% and inflation that topped 12%. The question remains, therefore, what would have become of Gerald Ford if he had given voters an alternate, compelling economic storyline?

Ford, however, didn't give them that other storyline and the Republican Party, in the meantime, still had no strong separate identity from the Democrats - unless you consider spending a little less than the Democrats wanted (Ford vetoed an average of 26.4 bills per year which is one way to be the *Party of No*) and taxing along with the Democrats as passing for a political identity. In that same November of 1976, the Democrats claimed 292 House seats – their second highest total since the Roosevelt years – and 61 Senate seats.

Taking Stock ~ Part I

As we take stock of the two decades we have just reviewed, it is hard to ignore the pattern that emerges. Again, the cautious manager Eisenhower, perhaps the father of *affordable* tax cuts, laid claim to a Republican majority in the House and Senate at the beginning of his presidency. However, as he presided over marginal tax rates of 91%, erroneously designed to satisfy the needs of government at the expense of individual initiative, Eisenhower endured three recessions and eventually gave way to the pro-growth/pro-citizen Kennedy Democrats. By 1964, factors which included the Kennedy/Johnson marginal rate tax cuts program helped build a 295 to 140 Democrat majority in the House. Once enacted, the tax cuts would soon have the economy booming.

By 1968, however, the Democrats' disarray under Johnson, which included a muted voice for pro-growth policies along with anti-war protests, led to the election of Nixon and a temporary narrowing of the divide. But the pro-government, anti-growth/tax and spend policies of the Republicans from 1969 to 1975, along with Watergate, once again cemented the

Republicans' minority status, 291 seats to 144 seats, as the chart below displays.

As anyone can plainly see, from the chart on the accompanying page, the largest Republican losses occurred during Eisenhower's and Nixon's government-centric, anti-growth administrations and when Republicans opposed or were ambivalent about pro-growth policies, i.e. the Kennedy's tax cuts.

Party Divisions in the House of Representatives From 1953 to 1977

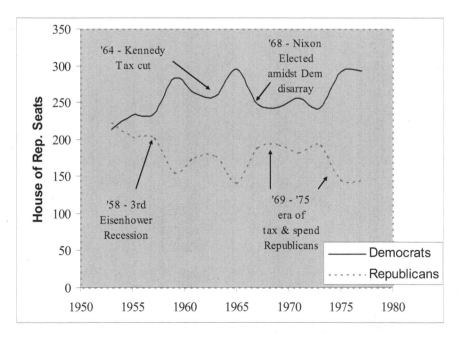

The Senate elections followed a similar pattern during the same period. The Democrats reached a high of 64 seats during the second Eisenhower recession and then bettered that by winning 67 seats in the 1962 election and 68 seats in the 1964 election, i.e. during the time of the Kennedy pro-growth policies.   Republicans would close the gap amidst the Democrats' disarray in the late 1960s but would squander their gains with tax and spend policies.   Those failed policies and Watergate would lead to the Democrats claiming 61 Senate seats in the 1974 election.

US Senate Breakdown from 1953 to 1977

Such political fortunes would change, however, with a grand curve on a cocktail napkin and a *Great Communicator*.

Chapter 3

Hope Matters

"A Leader is a Dealer in Hope"
Napoleon

"We are too great a nation to limit
ourselves to small dreams."
Ronald Reagan

Historians have sometimes quarreled as to whether the man creates the times or the times create the man. As the close of the seventies drew near, if nothing else, it was apparent that Ronald Reagan was the right man at the right time.

The late sixties and seventies brought the United States unprecedented challenges, social upheaval, unwanted new vocabulary and perhaps worst of all, a sense of diminished expectations. The Vietnam War separated the Country like no other war since the Civil War. The Pentagon Papers and the Watergate Cover-up challenged people's faith in their government. "Stagflation" entered the public lexicon in earnest along with something called the "*Misery Index*"[15] and an "Islamic Fundamentalist" revolution that held Americans hostage.[16]

For the prior sixteen years, the Nation endured an extended period of less than inspiring presidents – all of whom *managed* government to achieve social ends: Lyndon Johnson, who declined to run for a second term, Richard Nixon who resigned, President Ford – a president never elected, and then Jimmy Carter, who endured a hostage crisis helplessly and then watched, if not directed our Nation into a period of national malaise.

The 1980 election would change all that. In much the same manner that JFK's election reinvigorated the Nation after three recessions under Eisenhower, Ronald Reagan's election offered a wearied Nation a fresh start from Carter's malaise.

The Language of Despair Replaced by Hope

[15] Republicans referred to the combination of the unemployment and inflation indexes under President Jimmy Carter as the "Misery Index." Under Carter, unemployment topped 7% and inflation rose above 13%. The prime interest rate reached a high of 21.5%.

[16] Under President Jimmy Carter, the US embassy in Iran was overtaken by radical Iranian "students" who held Americans hostage for 444 days only to be freed as Reagan became president.

The near-complete unraveling of the Carter presidency occurred on the night of July 15, 1979. It was on that night that he gave his infamous "malaise" speech. Carter appeared to question Americans' resolve in a manner that seemed more appropriate to questioning his own. The seminal moment in his speech came when he said:

> "I want to talk to you right now about a fundamental threat to American democracy. I do not mean our political and civil liberties. They will endure. And I do not refer to the outward strength of America, a nation that is at peace tonight everywhere in the world, with unmatched economic power and military might.

> The threat is nearly invisible in ordinary ways. It is a crisis of confidence. It is a crisis that strikes at the very heart and soul and spirit of our national will. We can see this crisis in the growing doubt about the meaning of our own lives and in the loss of a unity of purpose for our Nation.

> The erosion of our confidence in the future is threatening to destroy the social and the political fabric of America."

By an electoral margin of 489 to 49, in November of 1980, the American people, however, decided that the erosion in confidence was in Jimmy Carter and replaced him with Ronald

Reagan.   Once again, American History was witness to a dramatic change in style, substance and spirit.

Despite precious little change in the economy or world affairs from the time of Carter's malaise speech, Reagan served notice in his 1980 address to his nominating convention that success was possible.   In reading these words, we must remember that leading up to the Reagan presidency, the succession of Johnson, Nixon, Ford and Carter produced such a loss in confidence in presidents that some skeptics doubted that the US or its presidency could be managed by just one person.

Unbowed by such skeptics, a confident Reagan turned about face from Carter's disappointments and, quoting Thomas Paine, declared: "We have it in our power to begin the world over again."

Reagan continued by stating:

> "Nearly 150 years after Tom Paine wrote those words, an American president told the generation of the Great Depression that it had a "rendezvous with destiny." I believe that this generation of Americans today has a rendezvous with destiny . . . The time is now, my fellow Americans, to recapture our destiny, to take it into our own hands."

Several months later, in his inauguration speech, Reagan continued his uplifting theme and summoned a Nation to greatness once again:

> "It is time for us to realize that we are too great a nation to limit ourselves to small dreams. We're not, as some

would have us believe, doomed to an inevitable decline. I do not believe in a fate that will fall on us no matter what we do. I do believe in a fate that will fall on us if we do nothing.

So with all the creative energy at our command, let us begin an era of national renewal. Let us renew our determination, our courage, and our strength. And let us renew our faith and our hope. We have every right to dream heroic dreams."

The difference between Carter's malaise rooted in failed government actions and Reagan's hope for individual Americans was not just a change in speechwriters. It was not just a change between a fallen president and a leader. It was a manifestation of Reagan's fundamental understanding that great leaders are *Dealers in Hope*, they are *Optimists* and they *engage their constituents in a higher purpose*. Such is the history of the great American Presidents George Washington and Abraham Lincoln.

Washington and Lincoln:
Leadership by Higher Purpose

Before the end of the Revolutionary War, there were those who wanted George Washington to become King of what would become these United States.[17]   But Washington, who was revered for his character, had a higher purpose – not just for himself, but for his Country. "Washington had the vision of an independent, republican, constitutional government controlled by a free people. He also envisioned this Nation as contributing to the uplifting and happiness in the years, even centuries, to come of the whole world."[18]

Indeed, Washington had great expectations for his Country:

> "As Mankind becomes more liberal, they will be more apt to allow that all those who conduct themselves as worthy members of the community are equally entitled to the protections of civil government. *I hope ever to see America among the foremost nations of justice and liberality.*"

As you read that again, please note Washington's use of the words liberal and liberality. He uses it in its original sense – the state of being free – not in the sense liberal Democrats would use it in the 1900s. Combined with his moral standing, it is little wonder that he became the Commander in Chief of the Continental Army, president of the Constitutional Convention and first president of the Country.

---

[17] *George Washington on Leadership* by Richard Brookhiser
http://www.pbs.org/n ewshour/gergen/brookhiser.html

[18] *George Washington, Genius in Leadership* by Richard C. Stazesky
http://gwpapers.virginia.edu/articles/stazesky.html

In accepting the latter, and relinquishing it after two terms, just as he relinquished his military power at the end of the Revolutionary War, Washington stood in the breach of *History*. He could have sought his own realm and thwarted the World's experiment with democracy – but instead, he remained principled, made the untested Constitution real, and with his brand of **Optimism** inspired the rest of *History*. It is for that leadership that Washington must be counted among *History's* absolute greatest.

That legacy of the first George W. is the same ideal that the current George W. wanted to foster when he dubbed the current century "the century of liberty."[19]   Long before Bush's Freedom Wars, however, Lincoln called upon a Country to save that ideal.

Lincoln Dies for the Last Best Hope

Contemporary Americans simply cannot know the magnitude of the difficulties that faced President Lincoln and, indeed, the young Nation. "By the time Lincoln arrived in Washington to be sworn in as the Nation's 16th president, 4 Mar. 1861, the Confederate States of America had been

---

[19] "I believe we're living in a century that will be called the century of liberty." President George W. Bush, on the 2004 campaign trial

formed."[20]   Lincoln rose to the office of the presidency after just a single term in the House of Representatives and a failed Senate run against Stephen A. Douglas.

In that short time, however, Lincoln had made more than a name for himself because of his opposition to the most divisive issue in American History: slavery – an issue that not only divided the Northern and Southern states – but also the Democrat Party into a Northern Faction and a Southern Faction.[21] Riding that division and his growing stature, Lincoln was elected president and some Southern states responded by seceding from the Union.

Thus, Lincoln was faced not with one crisis but two crises that were intertwined: (1) a fractured Country and (2) the growing chorus in favor of ending the horror of slavery - either of which would dwarf the problems of 2006 America.

Within weeks of his inauguration, the civil war began at Fort Sumter, Charleston Harbor, South Carolina. For over a year, the disparate sides fought America's most costly battles. In December of 1862, in his annual message to Congress, Lincoln called on his Nation not just to save the already fractured Union, but to an even higher purpose:

---

[20] Historical Times Encyclopedia of the Civil War,
http://www.civilwarhome.com/lincolnbio.htm.

[21] Just over 100 years later, a war would divide the Democrats again and lead to a Republican presidential victory. That war? The Vietnam War.

"Fellow-citizens, we cannot escape history. We of this Congress and this administration will be remembered in spite of ourselves. No personal significance, or insignificance, can spare one or another of us. The fiery trial through which we pass, will light us down, in honor or dishonor, to the latest generation.

We say we are for the Union. The world will not forget that we say this. We know how to save the Union. The world knows we do know how to save it. We—even we here— hold the power, and bear the responsibility.

In giving freedom to the slave, we assure freedom to the free—honorable alike in what we give, and what we preserve. We shall nobly save, or meanly lose, the last best, hope of earth."

It would be several years before the South's bid for independence and slavery were vanquished. In the end, Lincoln lost his life in the fight to give freedom to others. By persevering though the vicissitudes of a Civil War, he saved a Nation. By prevailing against slavery, he ensured not only his place in *History* as one of America's greatest presidents, but America's place in *History* as a place of justice and liberality - indeed the last best *hope* of earth.

It was not mere coincidence that Washington and Lincoln, in difficult times, called upon Americans to fight not just for the war at hand. Instead, Washington and Lincoln challenged Americans to look beyond themselves, to achieve something greater than the victory at hand. They inspired a young Nation to fight for and achieve justice, liberality, freedom and, of course, hope – not for them alone but for mankind as a whole. Those ideals, even though achieved with blood-soaked memories, were *positive* goals designed to lift up the Nation. Call it **Leadership By Higher Purpose**.

Although many other presidents have made reference to those ideals, Washington and Lincoln walk nearly alone because they shepherded a war-torn Nation through its most difficult hours – not by turning the concerns of the Nation inward, but instead, by challenging it to achieve a greater good.

Over a Century later, faced with crises of a different proportion, that lesson would not be lost on Ronald Reagan.

Chapter 4

Reagan Achieves Our Heroic Dreams

"We will be as a city upon a hill."
Ronald Reagan *quoting* John Winthrop

When the Reagan presidency began, the Nation was faced with economic troubles, a crisis in confidence and a decades-old Cold War.   When Reagan announced his candidacy for president, he placed blame for those problems not in the impossibilities of the time, but on the failings of its leaders:

> "The crisis we face is not the result of any failure of the American spirit; it is the failure of our leaders to establish rational *goals* and give our people something to order their lives by."

America, once again, has a president focused on goals and achievement. In his first Inaugural Address, Reagan asked the Nation to "renew our faith and our *hope*." Reagan was certain that, as a Nation, "*We have every right to dream heroic dreams.*" He also made it quite clear that "there [would] be no misunderstanding -- we're going to begin to act beginning today."

Rational goals would take the form of two broad initiatives designed as much to restore America's confidence as they were the political/economic problems of the day. Reagan proposed to invigorate the economy. He also proposed a military build-up. In time, it could fairly be said that both were designed to restore America, her standing in the World and to hasten the demise of the Soviet Union.

Reagan Takes on Economic Stagnation

If the economy was not working, it cannot be a surprise that Reagan chose to empower individual Americans to make it work - not more government programs. Thus, after thwarting an assassin's bullet on March 30, 1981, Reagan strode into a joint session of Congress just weeks later – an act that in-and-of-itself boosted America's confidence. He sought immediate action on his economic plan and declared:

"Our choice is not between a balanced budget and a tax cut . . . by attempting to reduce the deficit through higher taxes, [the budget] will not create the kind of strong economic growth and the new jobs that we must have . . .

Our across-the-board cut in tax rates for a three-year period will give [business] much of the incentive and promise of stability they need to go forward with expansion plans calling for additional employees . . ."

Reagan's words echoed Kennedy's words of two decades earlier. Recall Kennedy's words in response to Eisenhower's recessions:

"I repeat: our practical choice is not between a tax-cut deficit and budgetary surplus. It is between two kinds of deficits: a chronic deficit of inertia, as the unwanted result of inadequate revenues and a restricted economy; or a temporary deficit of transition, resulting from a *tax cut designed to boost the economy, increase tax revenues*, and achieve--and I believe this can be done--a budget surplus."

Reagan and Kennedy both faced a stagnant economy and both challenged America and called for the same private sector remedy: broad, marginal rate tax cuts. It is worthy to note that the marginal tax rate Reagan faced was the same marginal rate that the Kennedy/Johnson tax cuts set: 70%. In other words, in the intervening 20 years, no other president saw the wisdom of the Kennedy cuts and their expanded growth rates. Not coincidentally, three of those presidents were one term presidents or less, the other failed to finish his second term.[22]

There was a reason, of course, that Reagan chose to follow in Kennedy's footsteps and to seek broad tax cuts. For both men, tax cuts represented more than an economic policy. They represented a philosophy that believed in the inspirational power of freedom over the dulling limits of government. They both chose policies rooted in *Optimism* and that *Optimism* ignited our unbound spirits. Such is the power of granting economic freedom and why broad tax cuts are such a winning issue.

---

[22] It is also worthy to note that Johnson asked for passage of the Kennedy tax cuts after he complained that: "That tax bill has been thoroughly discussed for a year. Now we need action." Reagan's address to the joint session of Congress included a similar complaint: "It's been half a year since the election that charged all of us in this government with the task of restoring our economy . . . Six months is long enough. The American people now want us to act and not in half-measures." Finally, it is also worth considering that both the Kennedy and the Reagan tax cut proposals (a) were both initially met with significant skepticism and (b) were both passed in the wake of assassins' bullets and the sympathetic empowerment they engendered. Would those bills have passed in the absence of those bullets? One can only wonder.

A Cocktail Napkin and a Curve

It must be mentioned that the failings of those one-term presidents did not mean that the effects of the Kennedy tax cuts went unnoticed until Ronald Reagan ran for president. To the contrary, an intellectual movement was brewing from within and without the Republican Party and its story is important for Republicans to understand.

According to some, the take-off point of the movement occurred at dinner in December 1974. Art Laffer was with Donald Rumsfeld, then Chief of Staff to President Gerald Ford, Dick Cheney, then Rumsfeld's deputy, and Jude Wanniski. Art Laffer apparently grabbed a "napkin and a pen and sketched a curve on the napkin illustrating the trade-off between tax rates and tax revenues." [23]

According to Laffer, "Wanniski named the trade-off 'The Laffer Curve.'"[24] Wanniski describes the theory behind the curve as akin to the law of diminishing returns: "Raise tax rates too high and commerce will be stifled to the point that tax

---

[23] "The Laffer Curve: Past, Present, and Future" by Arthur B. Laffer, http://www.heritage.org/Research/Taxes/bg1765.cfm - a definitive article on the Laffer Curve and the effects of tax cuts.

[24] Ibid.

revenues will decline. At that point a reduction in tax rates will stimulate commerce and revenues will rise." [25]

The prized drawing took this shape:

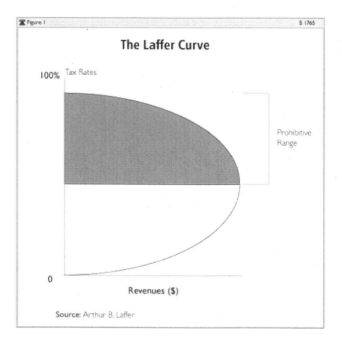

According to Laffer, there is an "economic effect" to cutting taxes, "a *positive* impact that lower tax rates have on work, output, and employment -- and thereby the tax base -- by providing incentives to increase these activities. Raising tax

---

[25] "The Laffer Curve: Past, Present, and Future" by Arthur B. Laffer, http://www.heritage.org/Research/Taxes/bg1765.cfm - a definitive article on the Laffer Curve and the effects of tax cuts.

rates has the opposite economic effect by penalizing participation in the taxed activities."[26]

Put another way, they gave people incentive to achieve.

~   ~   ~

Jude Wanniski blamed the woes of the 1970s on rising taxes. He writes that:

"The temporary, but sharp decline of the US economy in the 1970s was the result of the failure of our political leaders to realize the law of diminishing returns was eroding the economy in a new and different way . . .

We were inflating our way up the progressive tax schedules of the income-tax code. Robert Mundell and Arthur Laffer were the first economists on earth to realize that basic fact and to predict the bad things that followed."[27]

According to Laffer though:

"The Laffer Curve . . . was not invented by me. For example, Ibn Khaldun, a 14th century Muslim philosopher, wrote in his work The Muqaddimah: "It should be known that at the beginning of the dynasty,

---

[26] "The Laffer Curve: Past, Present, and Future" by Arthur B. Laffer, http://www.heritage.org/Research/Taxes/bg1765.cfm - a definitive article on the Laffer Curve and the effects of tax cuts.

[27] SSU Spring Lesson #4: "The Laffer Curve" by Jude Wanniski, http://www.wanniski.com/showarticle.asp?articleid=4167

taxation yields a large revenue from small assessments. At the end of the dynasty, taxation yields a small revenue from large assessments."

Laffer also points to:

"A more recent version (of incredible clarity) was written by John Maynard Keynes:

'Nor should the argument seem strange that taxation may be so high as to defeat its object, and that, given sufficient time to gather the fruits, a reduction of taxation will run a better chance, than an increase, of balancing the budget.

For to take the opposite view today is to resemble a manufacturer who, running at a loss, decides to raise his price, and when his declining sales increase the loss, wrapping himself in the rectitude of plain arithmetic, decides that prudence requires him to raise the price still more--and who, when at last his account is balanced with nought on both sides, is still found righteously declaring that it would have been the act of a gambler to reduce the price when you were already making a loss."[28]

Regardless of the origin of the curve, even Laffer's critics would come to say that "Professor Laffer is both the creator and the catalyst of the taxpayers' revolt that is sweeping America . . . he is its intellectual leader . . . [and no] serious examination of

---

[28] The Laffer Curve: Past, Present, and Future by Arthur B. Laffer, http://www.heritage.org/Research/Taxes/bg1765.cfm referencing John Maynard Keynes, The Collected Writings of John Maynard Keynes (London: Macmillan, Cambridge University Press, 1972).

America's current economic problems, and no significant proposal for tax cuts or tax reform, can fail to include an analysis of the Laffer curve."[29]

Republican appreciation of the Laffer curve, tax cuts and their political/economic implications, however, did not start with Ronald Reagan. That honor belonged, in large degree, to Congressman Jack Kemp and Senator William Roth, who introduced their tax cutting measure in 1977.[30]

According to Bruce Bartlett:

"Kemp and Roth thought that this sharp rise in tax rates [during the '60s and '70s] was largely responsible for the stagnation of the American economy in the 1970s."[31]

Bartlett aptly describes the debate between the emerging pro-growth movement and those inclined to what Kennedy would describe as "intellectual inertia."

"At the time the Kemp-Roth bill was introduced, however, the dominant view among economists was that

---

[29] A Comment on the Laffer Model by Max Moszer,
http://www.cato.org/pubs/journal/cj1n1/cj1n1-2.pdf

[30] Kemp-Roth Changed American Economic Policy, Bruce Bartlett,
http://www.ncpa.org/edo/bb/2002/bb071502.html

[31] Kemp-Roth Changed American Economic Policy, Bruce Bartlett,
http://www.ncpa.org/edo/bb/2002/bb071502.html. Note that even though tax rates stayed essentially the same, bracket creep pushed the effective tax rates of Americans higher.

budget deficits were the primary cause of inflation. They favored tax *increases*, not tax cuts, and said that passage of the Kemp-Roth bill would be dangerously inflationary.

Kemp and Roth responded that inflation resulted from the Federal Reserve creating too much money,[32] not deficits, and that a tight monetary policy, which they supported, would reduce inflation regardless of how large the deficit was.

Such a view was absolute heresy in 1977. The Congressional Budget Office, for example, believed that the money supply had nothing whatsoever to do with inflation, and that cutting tax rates would add fuel to it.

CBO Director Alice Rivlin said that output would fall if tax rates were cut, because workers could work less and still get the same after-tax income."

In my many speeches, exposing that last sentiment garners much amusement. Yet back then, and even today, many on the Left believe it to be so – they cannot grasp the full power of incentives and people's desire to achieve.

History is, however, well aware of with whom Reagan sided in that debate. Indeed, it could be no surprise that Reagan opted for the policy that would have a positive, ***Optimistic*** impact and provide individuals with incentives. Well knowing Supreme Court Chief Justice John Marshall's famous

---

[32] A position long championed by the Nobel Prize winning economist Milton Friedman.

admonition: "The power to tax involves the power to destroy," Reagan "rejected the conventional view and supported Kemp-Roth, making it his principal campaign issue in 1980."[33]

Once elected, on August 13, 1981, Reagan signed into law the Kemp-Roth tax bill which came to be known as the Economic Recovery Tax Act (ERTA). Under the law, marginal income tax rates were reduced by 25 percent over three years and the rates were indexed for inflation to prevent "bracket creep," yet another word that Americans came to know in the late 1970s.[34]

Reagan, Laffer, Kemp & Roth Were Right – Once Again, the Party of *No* Was Wrong

Although the Reagan tax cuts passed, they did so with limited Democrat support. With that historic vote, however, the Republicans and the Democrats began the process of role

---

[33] "Kemp-Roth Changed American Economic Policy" by Bruce Bartlett, http://www.ncpa.org/edo/bb/2002/bb071502.html.   Two years prior, the California voters threw down the gauntlet of the tax revolt by passing Prop 13 – a property tax limiting measure that restricted increases in property taxes.

[34] The Bracket Creep of the 1970s was a function of rising inflation that pushed wages higher and therefore incomes into higher tax brackets. However, because inflation eroded the value of money and therefore it took more dollars to purchase the same products it did before, people were forced to pay higher taxes without making economic gains. In other words, people were paying higher taxes on higher income but had no greater purchasing power – indeed, many had less because of the higher taxes. Eventually, income taxes were indexed to inflation by Reagan to significantly reduce bracket creep.

reversal. Recall that Goldwater called the Kennedy tax cuts "gimmickry" and the Republicans thought the cuts, along with the Great Society spending, were reckless. In the early 1980s, the Democrats were against the Reagan tax cuts and claimed that the Reagan military spending was reckless – a complete reversal of roles.

In both cases, the party that supported tax cuts was right - the *Party of No* was wrong. When Kennedy cut marginal tax rates **for those in the middle and upper brackets, who can thereby be encouraged to undertake additional efforts and...invest more capital**:

- The economy grew by 5.8 percent in 1964, and by 6.4 percent in 1965 and 1966, the longest economic expansion to date, and as a result:

- In the four years following the tax cut, federal government income tax revenue increased by 8.6 percent annually and total government income tax revenue increased by 9.0 percent annually.[35]

- From 1962-1969, government revenue *increased* 6.4 percent a year, compared with 1.2 percent a year between 1952-1959.

---

[35] "The Laffer Curve: Past, Present, and Future" by Arthur B. Laffer, http://www.heritage.org/Research/Taxes/bg1765.cfm

- Between 1962 and 1969, investment grew at an annual rate of 6.1 percent, far higher than the 3 percent annual rate for 1959-1962.[36]

Not surprisingly, the Reagan record was similar - despite the much higher hurdle of the more negative effects of stagflation. How damaging was the buildup of stagflation from Nixon to Carter? "Over the four years prior to 1983, Federal Income Tax revenue *declined* at an average rate of 2.8 percent per year, and total government income tax revenue *declined* at an annual rate of 2.6 percent."[37]

The Reagan cuts changed everything:

- This economic boom lasted 92 months without a recession, from November 1982 to July 1990, the longest period of sustained growth during peacetime and the second-longest period of sustained growth in US history.[38]

- The average annual growth rate of real gross domestic product (GDP) from 1981 to 1989 *increased* to 3.2 percent per year, compared with 2.8 percent from 1974

---

[36] "Do Tax Cuts Effect the Economy?" National Center for Policy Analysis, http://taxesandgrowth.ncpa.org/hot_issue/growth/

[37] "The Laffer Curve: Past, Present, and Future" by Arthur B. Laffer, http://www.heritage.org/Research/Taxes/bg1765.cfm

[38]" The Real Reagan Economic Record: Responsible and Successful Fiscal Policy" by Peter B. Sperry, PhD, http://www.heritage.org/Research/Taxes/BG1414.cfm

to 1981 [Nixon, Ford, Carter] and 2.1 percent from 1989 to 1995 [Bush I, Clinton].[39]

- Total federal revenues *doubled* from just over $517 billion in 1980 to more than $1 trillion in 1990. In constant inflation-adjusted dollars, this was a 28 percent increase in revenue.[40]

The Second Part of Reagan's Economic Renewal:
Regulatory Reform

If the Democrats under Kennedy and Johnson had a formula for cornering the market on votes during the 1960s, it was by tax cuts and a large-scale increase in government handouts. Remember, as you look again at this Heritage Foundation chart that depicts federal spending, large-scale government was still a new occurrence in the United States when Johnson introduced his Great Society programs. At that time, a politician could sell

---

[39] Supply Tax Cuts and the Truth About the Reagan Economic Record by William A. Niskanen and Stephen Moore http://cato.org/pubs/pas/pa-261.html.

[40] The Real Reagan Economic Record: Responsible and Successful Fiscal Policy by Peter B. Sperry, PhD, http://www.heritage.org/Research/Taxes/BG1414.cfm. Critics will argue that Reagan also raised taxes and those increased tax rates led to more revenues. Without the initial cuts, however, the train would have never started rolling. Further, the higher rates retarded future growth and reduced future tax revenues over time.

the notion that government was here to help. Not so by Reagan's time.

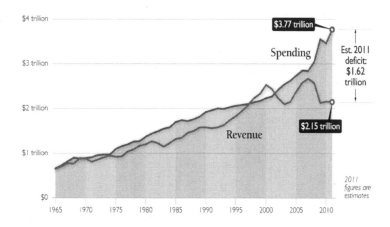

Indeed, one of Reagan's most memorable lines was: "The nine most terrifying words in the English language are 'I'm from the government and I'm here to help.'" Thus, by Reagan's time, although tax cuts were essential to his winning formula, increased government handouts were out of the question. The Reagan answer for the 1980s, and beyond, would be **Government Reform**.

President Reagan made his views on government quite clear in his Inaugural Address:

> "The economic ills we suffer have come upon us over several decades. They will not go away in days, weeks, or months, but they will go away. They will go away because we, as Americans, have the capacity now, as we have had in the past, to do whatever needs to be done to preserve this last and greatest bastion of freedom.

In this present crisis, government is not the solution to our problem. Government is the problem."

That was no mere "take away" line in a speech. To the contrary, by saying that, Reagan was signaling a seminal break in philosophy from presidents Hoover through Carter (excepting only Kennedy). Each of those intervening presidents grew government or raised tax rates in order to achieve political or social gains - perhaps none more visibly than *Republican* Richard Nixon with his combination of regulation, spending and tax increases. To those presidents, government was a constructive means to foster social ends and they became the proponents and managers of government.

Reagan had no such ambition. Reagan believed that government was *the* roadblock frustrating desired social gains. Reagan thought that government prevented average citizens from being able to improve their daily lives and the lives of those around them. Government did so by stifling initiative, by wasting resources and through excessive red tape.

So, rather than wanting to manage government, Reagan wanted to change the course of government, restore freedom and let the *American Spirit* lead us back to prosperity.

As such, faced with a downward spiral of government intervention that left the Country in economic trouble, Reagan moved to change the tide. In addition to cutting taxes, if the problem with government was excessive bureaucracy, regulations and their associated costs, what was the rational solution for the "Can Do" Reagan? Simple. Cut regulation, bureaucracy and costs.   So, at the very outset of his administration, President Reagan completely deregulated oil pricing which led to the end of the 1970's oil crisis. Perhaps the most visible step in that regard came in Reagan's first year when Reagan dismissed 13,000 government Air Traffic Controllers. In early 1982, Reagan called for a *New Federalism* – an effort to devolve power away from the federal government down to the states.

In the same year, Reagan established the Grace Commission - announced under the technical name of Private Survey on Cost Control – in an effort to root out government waste. Reagan also took on the 3rd rail of American politics: Social Security. Reagan convened a Blue Ribbon panel headed by Alan Greenspan that resulted in a Social Security Reform bill.

With regard to regulations, under President Reagan, the Office of Management & Budget, or OMB, required strict cost-benefit analyses for all federal regulations. The banking system was deregulated along with the airline industry, the telecommunications industry and the energy industry to name a few – all with considerable Democrat opposition.

Those actions met with varied success but one thing became clear: Republicans became the voice for reform and for cutting red tape. Considerable elements of the Democrat Party, on the other hand, in a preview of the 1990's and early 2000's, fought those reforms at nearly every turn. Consistent with their stance on the Reagan tax cuts, they had become the *Party of No*.

In time, the Republican Party would reap the political gains from that economic growth and reform. For now, however, Reagan turned his attention, the Nation's attention and the World's attention to ending the Cold War.

Reagan Wins the Cold War through Confidence

The Cold War long preceded Reagan's tenure in politics – but he was determined that it would not out last him. In typical Ronald "it can be done" Reagan fashion, when "[a]sked by his first National Security Adviser, Richard Allen, what his Cold War strategy was, Reagan replied: "We win, they lose."[41]

Reagan served clear and plain notice, just months after the passage of his tax bill, that he was not confused as to the state of Cold War affairs. In a speech on November 18, 1981, Reagan laid bare the Soviet actions during the previous decade despite America's arm *reductions*:

- The Soviets steadily increased the number of men under arms. They now number more than double those of the United States.

- Over the same period, the Soviets expanded their real military spending by about one-third.

- The Soviet Union increased its inventory of tanks to some 50,000, compared to our 11,000. Historically a land power, they transformed their navy from a coastal defense force to an open ocean fleet, while the United States, a sea power with transoceanic alliances, cut its fleet in half.

- During a period when NATO deployed no new intermediate-range nuclear missiles and actually withdrew 1,000 nuclear warheads, the Soviet Union deployed more than 750 nuclear warheads on the new SS-20 missiles alone.

In the face of that build up, the Left begged the new president to reach a deal with the Soviets. It was the American

---

[41] "The Gipper's Gift" by John Wohlstetter, http://www.discovery.org/scripts/viewDB/index.php?command=view&program=Technology%20and%20Democracy&id=2090

Left's claim that the Soviet build-up was justifiable because of its insecurity brought on by American policies. Such "Blame America First" psychology – if the Soviets are doing something wrong it must be because we were doing something wrong first – would become a staple of Democrat leadership and hasten the party's' reversal of fortunes.

Reagan, however, rejected the policies designed to effectuate a draw – such as containment and détente. Instead, Reagan sought to have the West *transcend* the Soviet Union.[42] In doing so, Reagan adopted an ***Optimistic*** goal for the West to achieve – not the morally **"equivalent"** tie the Left seemed so desperately to want.

According to Newt Gingrich, "the new president set his sights on the *higher goal* of freeing Russia and Eastern European countries from the Communist yoke."

Could Washington and Lincoln be disappointed in such leadership or its theme? Reagan well understood ***Leadership by Higher Purpose*** and couched this battle of the Cold War in moral tones easily appreciated by all but the most hardened. He served notice of that theme in his 1981 Inaugural Speech when he stated:

---

[42] "The West won't contain communism. It will transcend communism. We will dismiss it as some bizarre chapter in human history whose last pages are even now being written." Ronald Reagan 1981.

"Above all, we must realize that no arsenal, or no weapon in the arsenals of the world, is so formidable as the will and moral courage of free men and women. It is a weapon our adversaries in today's world do not have."

The next year, speaking to the British Parliament, Reagan predicted that if the Western alliance remained strong it would produce a "march of freedom and democracy which will leave Marxism-Leninism on the ash heap of history."[43]

In other words, Reagan had the temerity to voice what was obvious to all but the Left: that the Soviet system, because it was not based on freedom, was inferior and would therefore eventually fall. It was indeed the Evil Empire – we were not – and good would prevail.

Thus, Reagan had laid out an uplifting vision for the Country and the World. He defined the battle in terms of freedom and democracy versus repression and dictatorship. Now all that was needed were *rational steps* to achieve his *rational goals*.

According to Dinesh D'Souza, a **New Conservative**, "Reagan formulated the notion that the West could use the superior economic resources of a free society to outspend Moscow in

---

[43] "Russian Revolution, How Reagan Won the Cold War" by Dinesh D'Souza
http://www.nationalreview.com/flashback/dsouza200406061619.asp   [a definitive piece on the subject. Note the similarity in language and theme used by George W. Bush in his second inaugural speech. Dinesh D'Souza can certainly be described as a **New Conservative**.

the arms race, placing intolerable strains on the Soviet regime."[44] It also induced thoughtful people like Paul Craig Roberts to state that "few Americans realize that President Reagan's economic policy won the Cold War by rejuvenating Capitalism."[45] Roberts wrote that "Members of the Soviet Academy of Sciences, with whom I spoke in Moscow during the Soviet Union's final months, agreed that it was President Reagan's **confidence** in Capitalism, not his defense buildup that caused Soviet leaders to lose their confidence."

Even so, as D'Souza points out, History recorded that Reagan embarked on the largest peacetime military buildup on record. It remembers the *Reagan Doctrine* which challenged the Soviet Union on its fringes by supporting those trying to throw off the Soviet yoke in places near (like Nicaragua) and far (like Cambodia). Reagan even went so far as to say to Gorbachev's face: "We can . . . continue the arms race, which I think you know you can't win."

In a very real sense the Soviet Union couldn't win that war and Reagan's refusal to give up on SDI was perhaps a final straw in that regard. Not only did the Soviet Union lose its

---

[44]Same.

[45] "How an Actor Changed the World," Washington Times, June 7, 2004, http://www.washingtontimes.com/commentary/20040606-101646-4699r.htm.

confidence but it also lost the Cold War - an eventuality that Henry Kissinger described as "the most stunning diplomatic feat of the modern era."[46]

Perhaps what is most stunning about the victory was that it was won, as Margaret Thatcher put it, "without firing a shot." In other words, Reagan ended the Third World War, not with a full-scale war and all its negative implications, but, instead, by restoring **Optimistic** leadership designed to promote liberty.

In doing so, Reagan could rightfully claim a place alongside America's great presidents.

---

[46] "Russian Revolution, How Reagan Won The Cold War" by Dinesh D'Souza
http://www.nationalreview.com/flashback/dsouza200406061619.asp

Chapter 5

The Three Pillars

**"Successful political paradigms coalesce a party's base,
attract Independents and capitalize on divisions
in the opposing party."**
Thomas Del Beccaro

As the 1970s came to a close, voters were besieged with poor economic times and high taxes. They were also dispirited at home and with America's standing in the World. By the end of the 1980s, all of that was reversed. President Reagan, by championing freedom over government intervention, inspired Americans, restored their resolve, purpose and economic prosperity. Along the way, he started a political realignment the remnants of which can still be seen today. That realignment can be called *The New Conservative Paradigm – a paradigm supported by three Pillars*.

Reagan's pro-growth policies were central to his *Optimism* and his success. They formed the first **Pillar** of *The New Conservative Paradigm.* Prior to Reagan, only Republicans Harding and Coolidge and Democrats Kennedy and Johnson made dramatic cuts in income taxes and thereby invigorated the Nation. In between, Republicans Hoover, Eisenhower, Nixon, and Ford, along with Democrats Roosevelt, Truman and Carter opted for higher tax rates, slower economies and a less *Optimistic* Country.

In making dramatic income tax cuts – the center piece of the first **Pillar** - Reagan did not simply tell us that lower tax rates spur economic activity. While that is true, it is not an ideal - and while it makes good policy, it does not inspire generations to greater achievements - which inspiration is the responsibility of leadership.

Instead, Reagan had a *Higher Purpose* – he sided with the potential of the individual over the false promise of government. The magnitude of that change in governmental philosophy, and its effect today, cannot be overstated – and within that explanation lays the political power of **Pillar Number One**.

During the 1960s, when the Democrats were winning votes with programs, the average person believed that government programs could well be a force for good – and so Johnson,

Nixon, Ford and Carter ballooned government programs hoping for political success. By Reagan's time, however, the empty promises of government programs had been exposed and the reach of government had simply gone too far. Reagan tapped into the river of anxiety and frustration amongst the electorate that government, with its regulations and mandates, was an impediment to the ability of families and individuals to succeed.

Americans saw Reagan take on government and by doing so they felt he was restoring freedom to them. In a very real way, that is what **Pillar Number One** is all about. It is not merely some mathematical policy of lowering tax rates for which lip service need be paid. It is a liberating force because it ennobles the needs of individuals and families over government and recognizes the power of opportunity over the shackles of government dependency.

In becoming its champion, Reagan demonstrated his understanding of what President Coolidge said so long ago that the "wise and correct course to follow in taxation is not to destroy those who have already secured success, but to create conditions under which everyone will have a better chance to be successful."

Reagan's policies were also in keeping with Chief Justice John Marshall's telling words that "in a free government, almost all other rights would become worthless if the government possessed power over the private fortune of every citizen."

In other words, **Pillar Number One** *is nearly synonymous with freedom itself* and its sincere advocates are guardians of our freedoms. It is also plainly a policy of *Optimism* and a policy that inspires greater achievement.

Contrast that, if you will, with the *constant, negative* drumbeat of Democrat leaders to raise taxes – a policy that outright advocates *punishing* those who succeed and a policy that limits freedom. "Give me your vote and then we will take your money" – such is their demand. It is hardly the stuff of leadership and certainly not inspiring. Indeed rare is a time when government programs (other than perhaps war efforts) inspire a people to higher achievement. Such inspiration is only the domain of *Liberty* – an idea whose sworn adversary is government.

As a political matter, by the time Reagan got his tax cuts, he had coalesced Republicans behind his program. Many Independents supported his call to end bracket creep and to turn the economy around. The Democrats, for their part, were divided on the issue. By the end of the 1980s, and the 92 straight months of economic expansion, tax cuts were a powerful economic and successful political strategy that coalesced the Republican Party, attracted Independents and capitalized on the division within the Democrat Party.

In other words, Reagan's use of **Pillar Number One** was a success economically, politically and historically.

Pillar Number One, of Reagan's *New Conservative Paradigm,* was not without companions. Reagan exuded, if not personified, two other important characteristics that would play a key role in the construction of *The New Conservative Paradigm*. In what would become **Pillar Number Two**, in contrast to the Democrats growing self-doubt about America, Ronald Reagan unabashedly believed in America, its purpose and its defense. **Pillar Number Three** would become Reagan's counter to the Left's social revolutions: his *Respect for American Traditions and Values*. All were welcome tonics to a Nation wearied by the counter-culture years.

In doing so, President Reagan not only gave greater impetus to the emerging *New Conservative Paradigm*, but he also vanquished the negative vocabulary we came to know in the Carter years. President Reagan even engendered a new phrase of his own – *The Reagan Democrat* – and with that, the reversal in party fortunes drew closer.

Democrats Lend a Helping Hand
With Pillar Number Two
The Anti – "American Power" Wing Takes Hold

President Reagan believed in America, its purpose and its defense. He took pride in America and its traditions. Those beliefs were essential to defeating the defeatists of the prior four years. The Democrats, however, were not always defeatists.

To the contrary, Reagan's beliefs were not unlike President Kennedy's. He did not doubt America or its purpose or its defense. In fact, Kennedy still wanted the US to be the World's "arsenal of democracy." Kennedy sought "not merely peace for Americans but peace for all men and women -- not merely peace in our time but peace in all time." Kennedy's obvious reference to the mistaken pacifist Neville Chamberlain, who had declared "peace in our time" in reference to his meeting with Hitler just before World War II, made it very clear that his was an America of strength and purpose – a marked contrast to today's Democrat leadership and the Left in general. Indeed, Kennedy, as indicated by his authorization of the Bay of Pigs operation (his attempt to topple Castro), proved he was prepared to fight preemptively for freedom. Modern Democrat leaders, by contrast, sought an immediate withdrawal from Iraq and other places.

Kennedy's themes, in that regard, were traditional American themes. They were a proud heritage for a Country that had liberated Europe twice and South Korea within the previous forty-five years – a heritage celebrated by Kennedy and the Democrats when they had huge majorities in Congress.

With the loss of Kennedy, however, the tone of the Democrat Party changed dramatically as the 1960s progressed. In an ever so brief period of time, the Democrat Party became more than suspicious of American power and nearly contemptuous of its nature.

The obvious backdrop of the times was the Vietnam War. That War turned the Democrat Party, the Left, and the Media four square against the use of American power. The irony of that, of course, was that the Vietnam War was not fully engaged until Democrats Kennedy and Johnson made it so. Keep in mind that President Johnson "Americanized" the Vietnam War just three years earlier, in 1965, when he committed 90,000 troops to defeating the North Vietnamese.

The presidential election of 1968 placed that new-found anti-American power bias on display in front of a wide television audience. A year before the November election, an anti-war Senator named Eugene McCarthy of Minnesota announced he would run for president against a sitting pro-war incumbent, President Johnson. His remarkable success against Johnson, in the March 1968 New Hampshire primary, directly led to Johnson withdrawing from the 1968 presidential race on the last day of March, 1968.

Just before that, Senator Robert Kennedy joined the race for the White House on the Democrats side. Soon thereafter, Vice President Hubert Humphrey also joined the race. Kennedy and McCarthy were supported by the anti-war protestors they actively cultivated.

As the anti-war fever of their party grew to a pitch, the Democrats' convention in Chicago was marred by violent anti-war protests in August of 1968. The Nation, Democrats included, was taken aback. Hubert Humphrey became the Democrats nominee at that convention and in deference to the strength of the anti-war Democrats, one month before the election; Humphrey took the position that the Vietnam War had to end. He did so without a reference to, let alone an assurance of, the completion of the US mission.[47]

The anti-war movement culminated in some respects just four days before the election. In what appeared to be a concession to the anti-war movement that gripped his party,

---

[47] Much like the position many Democrats took on Iraq in the run up to the 2004, 2006 and 2008 elections.

President Johnson announced the suspension of the bombing of North Vietnam.

Four days later, Republican Richard Nixon completed his political comeback by defeating Democrat Hubert Humphrey.

In rather simple terms, the Democrats lost that election more than the Republican Nixon won that election. Remember that the Republicans were not offering a domestic agenda much different from that of the Democrats. The Republicans of the day, by in large, believed in tax increases and spending as did the Democrats. However, the Democrats, in a very short period of time and in a very public and startling way, tore their party asunder over **Pillar Number Two**: *Belief in America and her Defense*. They went from the pro-war establishment party to a divided anti-war party. In doing so, they were not appealing to American's desire to achieve or their faithful service to American ideals. To the contrary, in unprecedented fashion, they were saying to America that we were wrong.

It proved too much for voters to understand let alone support in sufficient numbers. As a result, the relatively unified Republicans, with the help of Independents, defeated those war-divided Democrats – just as they did in 1860 when the Democrats were divided over the Civil War and a relatively united Republican Party won. In that way, the election of 1968 proved the paradigm that "Successful political paradigms, coalesce a party's base, attract Independents and capitalize on divisions in the opposing party."

The anti-war conversion was a remarkable turnaround for the Democrats and the Left. After all, the Bay of Pigs took place under the watchful eye of the Kennedy administration just seven and one half-years before. Again, President Johnson "Americanized" the Vietnam War just three years earlier. Even the New York Times, in 1961, supported the use of American force in an editorial that:

> ". . . spoke of "communist aggression" against South Vietnam that had been "launched as a calculated and deliberate operation by the Communist leaders of the North." The editorial continued: "The outlook in South Vietnam certainly gives no basis for optimism . . . *Free World* forces, however, still have a chance in South Vietnam, and *every effort should be made the save the situation.*"[48]

Those lost echoes seem more than long ago and far away. They also were the last time the Democrat Party was ahead on **Pillar Number Two**.

To Mona Charen, a *New Conservative*, "[t]he Leftist critique of America's role in Vietnam set the tone for every

---

[48] *Useful Idiots*, by Mona Charen, p. 25, citing Norman Podhoretz' work, *Why We Were in Vietnam*. *Useful Idiots* is a remarkable book for anyone interested in an exhaustive history of Left's emerging and enduring "Blame America First" mentality.

Cold War debate that would follow for the next thirty-five years."[49]

Charen believes that:

> "The Left's explanation of America's participation in the war was cartoonish and grotesque. It featured the U.S. in the role of international outlaw, interfering in a civil war for the sole purpose of propping up a corrupt dictatorship that would do its bidding. Some radicals went further, arguing that the U.S. had sent troops ten thousand miles across the globe to secure mineral rights . . . for large American Corporations . . . [or that] the true reason for American intervention was 'to serve the economic interests of American businessman . . . [and] they painted the North Vietnamese and Vietcong as our *victims*."[50]

If you read that again, you can hear in those words a mantra repeated over and over again by the Left, and leading Democrats, whenever and wherever the US projected force abroad – whether it was in El Salvador, Nicaragua, Grenada, or in Iraq. No matter what the stakes, no matter what the nature of the enemy, a strong element of the Democrat Party was bound and determined to Blame America First.[51]   And if America was

---

[49] Id. at 28.

[50] *Useful Idiots* by Mona Charen, p. 28.

[51] It was a tone that stayed with a considerable wing of the Democrats that found voice once again in 2004 in Howard Dean. It was also on awkward display when John Kerry paraded Vietnam veterans in front of the camera as part of his 2004 acceptance speech.

to blame, the way to curb the appetite of the "military industrial complex" was to cut its funding.

In 1968, that mentality created an opening for the Republican Party to demonstrate that it was better suited to defend America – an opening not many years removed from when Lyndon Johnson used a "mushroom cloud" campaign ad to convince many Americans that Republicans and their Candidate Barry Goldwater were too dangerous to be trusted with the defense of America. Nixon, despite his shortcomings, exploited that opening to win the 1968 election.

Between 1968 and 1980, the succession of Democrat leaders, which included McGovern and Carter, did little to change their new identity with respect to **Pillar Number Two**. In 1980, after the failures of Carter, candidate and President Ronald Reagan seized upon that opening again to his and our great success. As we saw in the previous chapters, Reagan embraced America's historic ideals as expressed by Washington and Lincoln. Simply stated, Reagan wholeheartedly believed that America had a *Higher Purpose* and there was nothing for which America had to be ashamed. To the contrary, in full patriotic fashion, for Reagan America was a "shining city on the hill." Two large electoral victories appear to have demonstrated which view Americans preferred between the Democrats self-blame and Reagan's pride.

That Blame America First mentality, however, was not the only turn against traditional America that the Democrats took in the lead up to the Reagan years.

The Anti – "American Tradition" Wing Takes Hold

To the extent that a considerable wing of the Democrat Party would become identified as anti-American power during the 1960s and 1970s, other and similar elements of their Party took on traditional American life.

Note that prior to Reagan and the Reagan Democrat, it was no secret of American politics that the Democrat party was perceived as the champion of the workingman, blue-collar families and minorities. It was a perception long cultivated by a party that called Franklin Delano Roosevelt its own and was the forerunner of **Pillar Number Three**, *Respect for American Traditions & Values*.

That perception can be traced, in large part, to the Great Depression era - if not before. Many in America were convinced that the Great Depression was the fault of Capitalists and their playground of Big Business. It was also thought that Big Business was the domain of Country-Club Republicans and their party – a holdover from the days of Rockefeller and the industrial titans.

We know now that the cause of Great Depression was not Big Business but ineffective Big Government. In the lead up to the worst of the Great Depression, the Federal Reserve allowed the money supply to shrink by nearly $1/3$ and Congress did its part by enacting trade killing tariffs known as the Smoot-Hawley Act, and, of course, raising marginal tax rates.[52] Those acts, and others, turned a significant recession (which was caused in large part by the vagaries of Capitalism) into the Great Depression.

Nevertheless, at the time, and for years later, it was perceived as a result of the failings of Capitalism not the failings of government – failings which occurred on the watch of *Republican* Herbert Hoover. Given those perceptions, under a Democrat FDR, the national response to the Great Depression was not less government interference but, instead, more government interference.

The succeeding forty years reinforced those perceptions for many. They became a history whereby the Democrat Party purchased the loyalty of the less fortunate with a series of New Deals, Wars on Poverty and Great Societies. As we have seen, the Republican Party had no similar, or more importantly, *rival* agenda or theme with which to court the working class

---

[52] Congress also raised the top marginal income-tax rate from 24 percent to 63 percent after President Hoover persuaded them that "nothing is more necessary at this time than balancing the budget." As for the shrinking money supply, imagine if nearly $1/3$ of your assets or income suddenly were gone. Would you cut back on your spending? Perhaps decidedly so? The America of the '30s certainly answered that question decidedly so and many lost their jobs and little to no money to spend.

electorate.   That changed under Reagan but not without significant help from the Left and their party, the Democrats.

~ ~ ~

As we review this history, we would do well to remember the following from American historian Will Durant.   He surmised that tradition is to the civilization what memory is to the individual.   If the individual loses his memory - he is lost, so too for civilizations that discard their traditions too quickly - the American civilization included.   For much of America, that is the crux of the matter.   The pace and nature of the social change pushed by the Left is too much for their sensibilities – especially when the Left demands more than tolerance – they also want Americans to change their lifestyle, their school books and often times their most cherished beliefs.   Such demands are not easily met socially or politically.

So, as the American standard of living rose during the 60s, 70s and 80s, and families lessened their concern with economic issues and increased their concern with social stability, Middle America began to strike back.   Indeed, as our "Rosie The Riveter" and "Father Knows Best" idealism was replaced with "Anti-War Protests" and "Archie Bunker," the American Left, and the Democrats leaders that pander to them, caused a majority of Americans to recoil; to seek refuge for the dizzying pace of change – and to identify with a party and a leader that respected America, her traditions and values.

It was not an unnatural reaction. Often in history, when the traditions of a group are threatened, the group reacts by closing ranks and clutching ever tighter to their customs and beliefs – just like individuals who become defensive when they are challenged or criticized. Such is the history of the last 40 years for many Americans and the dynamic that would lead to Republicans taking a lead on **Pillar Number Three**, *Respect for American Traditions & Values*.

Thus, although the media would have Americans believe otherwise, it can be fairly said that the Republican Party did not start a religious uprising to do battle with the Left. Nor did the Religious Right seek the battle that ensued. The awakening of the so-called Religious Right, in fact, was instigated by the Left which was far too antagonist and disrespectful to many Americans and their traditions. The Republican Party became the natural home to many of those people motivated by a desire to hold on to their beliefs and their traditions – which was no small incentive. Much of Reagan's success can be credited to the fact that he understood that dynamic and then worked with them to channel that motivation into a political force. Indeed, rather than threatening American traditions, Reagan respected them and publicly stood proudly by them.

In doing so, Reagan provided calm amongst the social storm on the Left. To this day, the Republicans benefit from that leadership in the form of increased vote totals and so many grassroots volunteers – all of which translates into a lead with respect to **Pillar Number Three**, *Respect for American Traditions & Values*. For their part, the Far Left continues to push the envelope farther and farther. Amidst such social arrogance, the Republicans can stay ahead if they continue to honor American values and traditions and if they remain the calm amidst the Left's social storm.

~   ~   ~

Most prominent in that agenda was the Left's desire to remove God from the Public Square – a predilection that struck at the hearts and imaginations of many Americans. And contrary to most American's understanding, it was a rather recent phenomenon.

As a practical matter, prior to FDR and his Supreme Court Packing plan, the federal government was simply not that large or that active. The States were the primary crucible of legislative and judicial action. FDR's New Deal, however, ballooned the size of the federal government. A suddenly larger federal government proceeded to grab power from the States on a variety of levels. In order to achieve those goals, Roosevelt devised his Court Packing Plan as a prelude to a power grab by the federal courts.[53]   Although Roosevelt was primarily concerned with expanding the power of the federal government over economic and regulatory issues, in time, the Left, and the Democrat Party in particular, would use the expanding powers of the federal courts to advocate social changes.

As part of that dynamic, issues we previously understood as "social issues" subject to social norms across a varied Nation were being "decided" by federal courts.   Lawsuits proliferated claiming that the acts occurring within a single state violated the US Constitution to the alleged detriment of everyone.   In that train arrived a series of Separation of Church and State/Establishment Clause cases heard in the federal courts. Many of those cases were driven by an express desire on the part of the Left to have public expressions of our religious culture, if not our history, stricken from the Public Square.

---

[53]   In 1937, after the Supreme Court struck down several key provisions of Roosevelt's New Deal, Roosevelt proposed expanding the Court from nine justices to fifteen and forcing the retirement of justices at age 70. It was an obvious ploy for Roosevelt to appoint judges who would support his expansion of federal power. In the face of Roosevelt's plan, two justices switched their votes and paved the way for Roosevelt's New Deal expansion of federal power. It must be noted that the rapidly expanding power of the federal judiciary was the realization of Thomas Jefferson's fear expressed by him in this quote: "The great object of my fear is the federal judiciary. That body, like Gravity, ever acting, with noiseless foot, & unalarming advance, gaining ground step by step, and holding what it gains, is ingulphing insidiously the special governments [i.e. the states] into the jaws of that which feeds them."

Of course, it is the belief of most Americans, however misguided, that the Founders erected the proverbial "wall" known as the Separation between Church and State. It is also widely assumed that that principle was preserved by our court system throughout our history. Honest history books, however, give a rather different account.

In fact, only *two* cases in the 150 years prior to FDR cited that notion of a Separation between Church & State[54] – one to uphold a law against polygamy in response to the polygamist's defense of a so-called religious right to do so[55] - and the other striking down an Oregon law that would have required all children to attend public school.[56]   Neither case could be characterized as anti-religious: the former striking down polygamy and the latter actually *preserving* the right of parents to send their children to *religious* schools.

Thus, for over 150 years, the federal courts left alone our religious heritage if not supported it. Why? Although too voluminous a topic to adequately handle in this book, in all likelihood it was because our cultural heritage of expressions of God in the Public Square were countless if not ubiquitous – they were an integral part of our culture. They stemmed from

---

[54] That fact and others like them are cited in an exhaustive history of this topic written by David Barton in his work *Original Intent, The Courts, the Constitution & Religion.*

[55] Reynolds v. United States, 98 US 145 (1878)

[56] Pierce v. Society of Sisters, 268 US 510 (1923)

the very birth of the First Amendment and, despite being under fire, they last until this day. Consider if you will that:

> "On the *same day* that Congress approved of the final wording of the First Amendment to the Constitution (Congress shall make no law respecting an establishment of religion or prohibiting the free exercise thereof), that same Congress passed a resolution "to wait upon the President of the United States to request that he would recommend to the people of the United States a day of public thanksgiving and *prayer, to be observed by acknowledging with grateful hearts the many signal favors of the Almighty God.*" Eight days later, Washington issued a proclamation that began "*Whereas it is the duty of all nations to acknowledge the providence of almighty God.*"[57]

Regardless of what you may have thought before, it is beyond reason to believe that the Founders expected the federal government to root out God from the Public Square by approving of a provision "acknowledging . . . Almighty God" and a day of national prayer on the *same day* that they approved of the 1st Amendment.

The following historical facts strengthen that analysis:

- The first Supreme Court Justice John Jay, in response to a request about whether clergymen could attend regional functions of the Supreme Court wrote: "The

---

[57] *Original Intent, The Courts, the Constitution & Religion* by David Barton

custom in New England of clergyman's attending should in my opinion be observed and continued."[58]

- In 1800, the US Congress authorized the Capitol to be used as a Church building and three years later John Quincy Adams confirmed his attendance to such proceedings in his diary.[59]

- When the Capitol was rebuilt, after the British burned it in 1814, in the House chambers a series of reliefs were placed on the walls around the entire chamber. All of the reliefs were profiles except one: the relief that directly faces the podium - from which the State of the Union is given. Whose relief looks directly upon the legislators as they deliberate? Moses.

- In 1864, so many years after the First Amendment was adopted, that the phrase "In God We Trust" first started appearing on US currency after an act of Congress that year – a practice which continues to this day.

The state courts acted in concert with those traditions. Consider this passage from *Religion in the United States of America*, Rev. R. Baird, 1844, Blackie and Son, Publishers, p. 275, about an 1812 criminal case:

"A person was indicted at New York . . . for aspersing the character of Jesus Christ, and denying the legitimacy of his birth. He was tried, condemned, fined, and imprisoned. On that trial chief Justice Kent, still living, and thought second to none in the Country in point of legal knowledge, expressed himself as follows:

---

[58] Id.

[59] Id.

'The people of this state, in common with the people of this country, profess the general doctrines of Christianity as the rule of their faith and practice; and to scandalize the Author of these doctrines is not only, in a religious point of view, extremely impious, but, even in respect to the obligation due to society, is a gross violation of decency and good order.'

Nothing could be more offensive to the virtuous part of the community, or more injurious to the tender morals of the young, than to declare such profanity lawful.

It would go to confound all distinction between things sacred and profane . . . No government . . .among any of the polished nations of antiquity, and none of the institutions of modern Europe (a single minority case excepted), ever hazard such a bold experiment upon the solidity of the public morals, as to permit with impunity, and under the sanction of their tribunals, the general religion of the community to be openly insulted and defamed . . .

True, the Constitution has discarded religious establishments. It does not forbid judicial cognisance of those offenses against religion and morality which have no reference to any such establishment, or to any particular form of government, but are punishable because they strike at the root of moral obligation, and weaken the security of the social ties.

To construe it as breaking down the common-law barriers against licentious, wanton, and impious attacks upon Christianity itself, would be an enormous perversion of its meaning."

How could a judge, claimed by at least one to be *"second to none in the country in point of legal knowledge,"* render such a decision over 20 years after the passage of the First Amendment to the Constitution? Quite simply, because it was in keeping with the American culture, then and even now.

It was that tradition the Left took on with a series of cases that struck at the heart of America's religious heritage.   As David Barton points out, the assault has been relentless:

- numerous cases in the 1960s and 1970s against prayer in school

- a 1965 case holding that freedom of speech was guaranteed to students unless the topic is religious

- a 1976 case holding that it was unconstitutional for a Board of Education to use or refer to the word "God"

- a 1979 case holding that it was unconstitutional for kindergarten teacher to ask whose birthday is celebrated by Christmas[60]

Quite simply, if it was not unconstitutional for church services to be held in the US Capitol, in what sense is it unconstitutional for prayer to occur in a school?   If Washington, who knew something of the founding of our Country, could establish a day of Thanksgiving to the Almighty God, in what sense was it unconstitutional for a public official to refer to the word God?

---

[60] *Original Intent, The Courts, the Constitution & Religion* by David Barton

For many Americans then, and now, there simply was no logical answer to those questions and others like them. In response to years of such legalistic and other attacks on their way of life, if not their heritage, significant parts of the Country, including those so pejoratively referred to by the Media as being in the Bible Belt, took considerable offense, mobilized and became the Religious Right.

Candidate Ronald Reagan agreed with them and the Democrat's once Solid South, populated with Evangelical Christians, agreed with him. In the 1980 general election, Republican Ronald Reagan carried the South (excluding Georgia). It would soon become the Solid Republican South that it is today. But that was not all.

Though it had attacked America's history as a liberator and its religious traditions, the Left was not yet finished. The social fabric of America was stretched to the point of tearing, on a number of other issues as well, leading up to Reagan's election and beyond.

The Left's and the Democrat's favorite method for change seemed to become lawsuits. Unhappy with the pace of "progress" afforded them by legislators and presidents, let alone ever emancipating technology, lawsuits were used to secure "rights."

Civil rights cases abounded and the case that changed the Unites States forever was *Griswold v. Connecticut* - a case decided in 1965 by the US Supreme Court. It established a "zone of privacy" that was hitherto unknown. In time, that "zone of privacy" would lead to perhaps the most famous Supreme Court decision of the latter half of the 20th Century: *Roe v. Wade.* That case too recognized a federal "right" that superseded "rights" not given in certain states. And with that case, the issue of *Life* was thrust with great verve square and center into American public life.

Outside the courts, for many in the Country, the dizzying pace of the 1960s was simply too much for the small town ideal to which they held. The 1970s & 1980s, filled with MTV, "R" rated movies, teen pregnancies and the like provided them little in the way of relief. Although the American historical philosophers Will and Ariel Durant could leisurely question whether:

> "The moral laxity of our times is a herald of decay rather than a painful or delightful transition between a moral code that has lost its agricultural basis and another that our industrial civilization has yet to forge into social order and normality . . ."[61]

For many Americans, whose simple ambition was to have their children's childhood be as innocent as theirs, the assault

---

[61] *The Lessons of History* by Will & Ariel Durant

on their sensibilities and values was simply too much – and played no small role in the rise of the Religious Right – a political force that cemented **Pillar Number Three**, *Respect for American Traditions & Values* in Reagan's favor.

Indeed, the candidate and then President Ronald Reagan alternatively fostered and echoed their sentiment. Quite simply, amidst such turmoil and moral relativeness, he represented a nostalgic view of America – one of strength and honor.

Put another way, President Reagan, and in time, the Republican Party, in addition to its pro-growth policies, became the political protectors of God and Country. That dynamic also marked the evolution of **Pillar Number Three** from concern for working families to the preservation of the traditional ideals and values cherished by Middle America. The Democrats, along with their counterparts in Hollywood and the Media completed the 1980s with a disdain for such concepts.

Nearly a quarter century later, in the form of NASCAR Dads, the Evangelical vote, the transitioning Catholic vote and more, the reversal in fortunes for the Parties on **Pillar Number Three**, *Respect for American Traditions & Values*, remains prevalent. It speaks to many soccer moms and families now concerned with social stability - and is no small key to *The New Conservative Paradigm*.

Taking Stock ~ Part II

We have now progressed through the 1970s and into the late 1980s. The reversal in fortunes of the parties on issues was nearly complete and the Republican majority would not be far off.

Before we move on, let us briefly revisit our chart from before and rename a segment to incorporate our new understanding of the Democrats' disarray in the late 1960s. Surely the factors that persuaded Johnson's decision not to seek re-election caused great difficulty for his party. Amidst the Vietnam War, divisions in his party abounded.

The Republicans were certainly able to capitalize on that dynamic. But as we have seen, for the first time, and in a fashion dramatically different from Kennedy, the Democrats turned against America, its ideals and some of its traditions. The intensity of that turn at least partially explains how the Democrats lost the White House – along with their party divisions and their abandonment of pro-growth ideals.

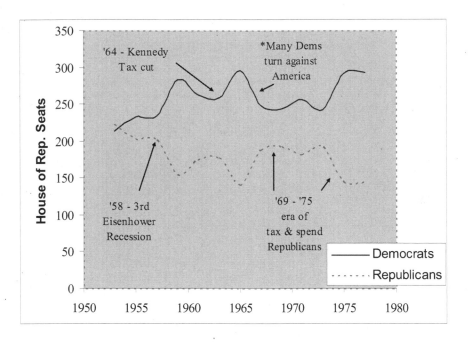

In the prelude to the Nixon Election in late 1968, we can see now that the Democrat Party no longer spoke of tax cuts or growth. To the contrary, the election was fought on the issue of the war and many Democrats spoke out virulently against America and its values. That produced an opening for Republicans. Although the Republicans became the party identified with a strong national defense, unfortunately Republicans did not grab the pro-growth mantle. As a result, neither Nixon nor Ford were celebrated for their economic policies.

As we have seen, those failings led to Carter.   Reagan, however, truly began the process of making the Republican Party the Majority Party.

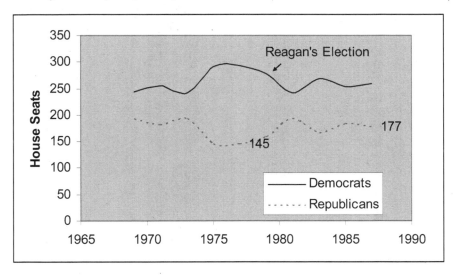

Under President Reagan, the Republicans narrowed the gap in Congress. The party recovered from their low of 145 seats in the House.   They reached a high of 192 seats with his first election but fell back 10 seats with the difficulties of Iran-Contra and after *raising* taxes in 1985.

Also under Reagan, the Republican Party actually became the Majority Party in the Senate for the first time since 1953 - before the Iran-Contra affair and a series of non-income tax increases[62] would cost Republicans their majority.

---

[62] In 1983, Reagan agreed to raise the Social Security tax rate. In 1984, Reagan raised taxes again by signing the Deficit Reduction Act of 1984. Those increases and the negative drag on the economy associated with them, however, did not come close to offsetting the benefits of the massive income tax reductions. Even so, they were not helpful politically.

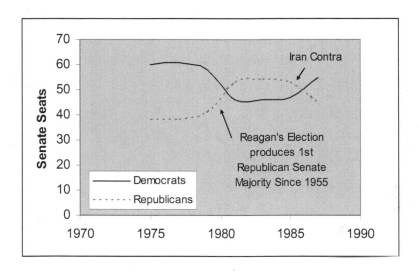

However, under Reagan, the parties had largely reversed their roles. The Republicans now stood for what would become *The New Conservative Paradigm*:

- Pillar Number One: Pro- Growth Policies including cutting taxes and government reform

- Pillar Number Two: Belief in America, its Purpose and its Defense

- Pillar Number Three: Respect for American Traditions and Values

All of those positions could rightfully be identified with John F. Kennedy during the early 1960s and produced considerable majorities for the Democrats in the early and mid-

1960s. The Democrat leaders, on the other hand, in the late 1980s stood for:

- Raising taxes
- Skepticism of America and weak on defense
- Callousness, if not contempt, towards American Traditions and Values

The first of those current Democrat positions, raising taxes, could more or less be identified with the Republicans in the early and mid-1960s. As we saw, Republicans opposed the Kennedy tax cuts and the Democrats were therefore ahead on **Pillar Number One**. As for national defense, Johnson successfully painted the Republicans as untrustworthy leaving the Democrats ahead on **Pillar Number Two**. And, as we have seen, dating back to the New Deal if not beyond, the Democrats, up until Reagan, had a stronger hold on **Pillar Number Three**, concern for the working family.

Reagan reversed all of that. However, the next two US presidents failed to heed any of Kennedy's or Reagan's lessons on how to focus a Nation on achievement through private initiative. As a result, one became a one-term president and the other, despite his tri-angulations, would cause his party to endure unprecedented losses in Congress – such are the stories of the first President Bush and William Jefferson Clinton.

Chapter 6

Bush 41 & Clinton: The Years of Lost Opportunity

"He who refuses to embrace a unique opportunity loses the prize as surely as if he had failed."
William James

The enormous success of the Reagan presidency was not without its legacies. America and its economy recovered. The end of the Cold War was near. Tax cuts became more than just a policy tool; they became an inspirational force and the new fault line in American politics. Party affiliation began to change along with the balance of power in Congress.

The Presidencies of George Herbert Walker Bush and Bill Clinton, however, seemed to ignore the lessons of the past. As a result, both Presidencies represent missed opportunities for their Parties. As a statistical matter, we can see that the presidency of George Herbert Walker Bush, or Bush 41, did little to improve the Republican fortunes in Congress. The presidency of Bill Clinton, on the other hand, did great things for Republicans.

The Bush 41 & Clinton Years

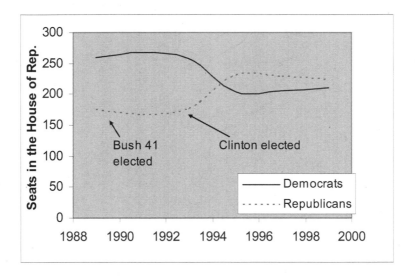

Conventional wisdom, of course, would lead us to believe that the presidency of Bush 41 should have led to more Republicans in Congress and the presidency of President Bill Clinton would have led to more Democrats. Why they did not was just one more step towards the cementing of *The New Conservative Paradigm.*

The Factors That Were Constant

Of the Pillars we are following (1) Pro-growth Policies, (2) Belief in America, it Purpose and its Defense, and (3) Respect for American Ideals and Values, the latter two changed little during the Bush 41/Clinton years. If anything, they became more deep-seated.

Bush 41 Maintains the Republican
Lead on Pillar No. 2

By all accounts, it must be said that the successes of Bush 41 were not in the economic arena but in area of national defense and foreign policy. Bush 41 undertook many and varied actions that cemented the Republican Party's image as strong on defense:

1989

- Bush offers assistance to Poles in their election that ends the one-party Communist rulc

- Bush announces restrictions on China in response to the Tiananmen Square Crisis

- The Berlin Wall falls and Bush meets Gorbachev in Malta

- Bush removes Dictator Noriega from Panama

1990

- Bush signs Arms Reduction Agreement with Russia

- Bush sends troops to Middle East in response to Iraqi invasion of Kuwait

1991

- Operation Desert Storm frees Kuwait from Saddam Hussein.
- Bush signs Start I with Gorbachev

- The Soviet Union dissolves

1992

- Bush and Yeltsin declare an end to the Cold War and agree to reduce nuclear stock piles

- Bush signs arms treaties with the new Russian Republics

Few four-year periods in American History or World History could boast such successes. The fall of the Berlin Wall was a most demonstrable end to an era. The Republicans rightfully claimed and were given credit for winning the Cold War.[63] Beyond that, the diplomatic run up to Operation Desert Storm was a significant achievement during Bush 41's presidency – *except at home with Democrats of course.*

The Democrat Leadership Cements
Their Weak Defense Credentials

We can recall that when the Republicans were faced with the Kennedy/Johnson tax cuts in 1964, Republicans had a choice to either be *right* or to be *contrary*. They chose contrary and paid for that in Congressional elections for years. When it

---

[63] Despite such recognition, President Bush missed an opportunity to highlight the fall of the Berlin Wall – choosing instead to say we do not want to "gloat." It is a reluctance his son George W. Bush shares given his refusal to tout the successes of his own presidency.

came to liberating Kuwait, the Democrats also chose to be contrary and pay for that decision to this day.

When Iraq invaded Kuwait, the Democrats held a majority in the US Senate by a margin of 55 – 45. The vast majority of those Democrats, 45, voted **against** Operation Desert Storm. According to Senator Robert Dole, "Desert Storm's defeat in the US Senate would have been one of history's most serious blows against a president in a crisis."[64]

Nevertheless, the voices of the Senate Democrats confirmed that for many, the Democrat Party was little changed from 1968. As you read these quotes by Senate Democrats made during the Senate debate on whether to authorize Desert Storm, try to remember (1) that it was Iraq that invaded Kuwait without provocation, and (2) *that the UN Security Council, yes even the UN, already voted to authorize the use of force if Iraq didn't withdraw from Kuwait.*

- "The president is wrong to have threatened Iraq with war."

- "President Bush appears to be on the verge of making a terrible mistake that will have tragic consequences for the whole world."

- "The administration is making a great mistake."

---

[64] "The Tough Choices," Robert Dole's Wall Street Journal from March 13, 2001

- "War would be a tragic mistake."

- "We are on a disastrous course."

- "The rush to combat now . . . is . . . tragically shortsighted."

- "The president . . . has moved in the wrong direction."

- "We are going to make such a tremendous blunder."

- "The president is marching this country toward a senseless and unnecessary war."

- *"The president should retreat* 'back to the defensive positions of the period up to Nov. 8th." [65]

Less than two months after those defeatist comments by Democrat US Senators, in March of 1991:

- Iraq forces were gone from Kuwait

- Iraq accepted a cease fire and the American Troops were on their way home

- George Herbert Walker Bush's poll ratings were at 89%

As a result of Desert Storm, the Democrats had done nothing to change America's view as to which party believed in America and its Purpose and which party should be trusted with the national defense.   Despite such success, however, re-election would elude Bush 41 and the Republicans would not yet recapture Congress.

---

[65] http://thomas.loc.gov/cgi-bin/query/z?r102:S13MR1-328:

A Glaring Lesson in
Political Economics for Republicans

If Republicans had burnished their credentials on national defense during Bush 41 with some enormous successes, then what could explain Bush's loss to Clinton in the 1992 presidential election?   After all, there was no reversal on the issue of American Traditions and Values. Those values were still under attack by the Left. From the continuing efforts to remove God from the *Public Square* to whether the Pledge of Allegiance could be said in the classroom, and whether school prayer would be allowed were still issues of the day that motivated Middle America.   Beyond that, TV violence was of such concern that Congress passed legislation on the issue in 1990. The battles between pro-life forces and the abortion on demand crowd were, if anything, heating up *with the Left running to excess.*   They were highlighted when women's groups faulted Madonna for making a record that featured an unmarried young woman choosing not to end her pregnancy.[66] Such is the definition of going too far.

---

[66] In the song "Papa Don't Preach" and accompanying video, a young girl decides to keep her child. Madonna was faulted for not expressing the alternative in the song – a clear indication of Left's rising extremism on social issues which would be so prevalent in the 1990s.

In those ways and more, the Democrats were still antagonistic to traditional values and Middle America took affront and the Religious Right continued to flex its political muscle in response.

Thus, it is correct to say that on the issues of traditions and values and who better to defend America, nothing appreciable had changed – the Republicans were ahead on both issues.

What changed was George Herbert Walker Bush's mind on *taxes*. For many American voters that was unforgivable and *it serves as a critical if not defining lesson for Republicans on how to stay ahead*.

~ ~ ~

I can recall driving down a windy road in route to meet a client the night of Bush's acceptance speech at the Republican convention. It seems odd to me now that I could have missed watching that speech on TV but the radio experience provided its own rewards. For many Republicans and the Nation, there was an uneasy sense about the resolve of Bush 41. It was an uneasiness well taken given that he had branded Reagan's pro-growth policies as "voodoo economics" eight years before.

By most accounts, it was one of Bush 41's best speeches. The highlight of that speech, which came through that night for radio and television audiences alike, was a set of lines that would define his presidency rather than his significant achievements in foreign affairs:

> "I'm the one who will not raise taxes. My opponent, my opponent now says, my opponent now says, he'll raise them as a last resort, or a third resort. But when a politician talks like that, you know that's one resort he'll be checking into.
>
> My opponent won't rule out raising taxes. But I will. And the Congress will push me to raise taxes, and I'll say no, and they'll push, and I'll say no, and they'll push again, and I'll say, to them,
>
> **Read my lips: no new taxes.**"

There was no more memorable set of lines for Bush 41 that night or any other night. Even so, it was not the first time that Bush 41 had made the statement. The Republicans saw the effect the tax issue had during the Reagan-Mondale campaign. Mondale had made it clear that he would raise taxes and was crushed in the general election.

In an attempt to make that lesson orthodoxy for Republicans, in 1986, Grover Norquist, of the Americans for Tax Reform began promoting his "taxpayer protection pledge," which asked candidates to promise not to raise marginal tax rates on income. During the 1988 presidential primaries,

"George Bush pulled ahead of Bob Dole . . . by taking the pledge and bashing Dole for refraining."[67]

Those lessons were not lost on Bush's speechwriter Peggy Noonan who wanted to emphasize the pledge for political effect.   Jack Kemp, a co-author of Reagan's tax cuts and perhaps "the" political/economic conscience within the Republican Party at the time, advocated Bush's pledge because it was economically right.

Just over two years later, however, Bush 41 changed his mind and the course of national politics.

At issue was a rising deficit brought on by excessive spending.   The Democrats wanted a budget deal and the president wanted action. As an inducement to get President Bush to make a deal, the Democrats in Congress promised to trade spending cuts for new taxes.   In making that offer, the Democrats placed Bush in the same position as the Republican Hoover, the Democrat Roosevelt, the Republican Eisenhower, the Democrat Kennedy and the Republican Reagan. Should he raise tax rates or lower them to increase revenues?

On November 5, 1990, President Bush sided with government, Hoover, Roosevelt, and Eisenhower and became a manager of government instead of a guarantor of economic freedom. Bush made that deal and he signed a budget deal that

---

[67] "Our Enemy, The States: The federal Republicans are okay, but the governors need to get with it" by Ramesh Ponnuru, http://www.nationalreview.com/nrd/trial/p.php?i=20050411&v=t&a=636

included an increase in tax rates. It was touted as a deal that would reduce the budget deficit by $500 billion. The consequences would be real - but not as Bush intended.

Politically, it reignited the debate as to whether Bush 41 was a man of conviction and whether he was a true believer on the issue of pro-growth policies. Pat Buchanan made great hay of the flip flop in the lead up to his success in the New Hampshire primary and Clinton would do the same in the general election.

Economically, the budget/tax bill was more of a flop than Bush's flip on taxes:

- Just over a year later, in December of 1991 unemployment reached 7.1% as an outgrowth of a recession that began in 1990 – a recession exacerbated by Bush's tax increase.[68]

- The budget deficit for the year Bush signed the bill was $261.9 billion in Fiscal Year 1990 – *the lowest of his presidency*. Two years later, Bush ran the *highest* deficit of his presidency: $318.5 billion in FY 1992.

The Bush experience on raising tax rates should be a clear political and economic lesson to all Republicans – no less a lesson than the party should have learned under Eisenhower

---

[68] Remember, as Dr. Laffer would tell you, tax policy has more than an arithmetic effect on the economy. Tax cuts have a psychologically beneficial impact which spurs people to greater achievement. Tax hikes, quite understandably, have the opposite effect.

and Hoover.   First, Bush failed to heed Reagan's 1982 admonition that "We don't have a trillion-dollar debt because we haven't taxed enough; we have a trillion-dollar debt because we spend too much." As if to confirm Reagan's warning, the Democrats never made good on their spending cuts pledge to Bush.

More importantly, however, was this economic fact: **In the face of difficult economic times, raising tax rates does not result in higher tax revenues than otherwise would have been collected without the rate increase**.   Instead, as Larry Kudlow – a *New Conservative* - is fond of saying, it acts like a "wet blanket" and retards revenue growth over the long term. Ask Herbert Hoover who, obsessed with the deficit, raised the marginal income tax rate from 25% to 63% - a major contributing factor to the Great Depression.

Republican Governor Pete Wilson of California learned the same lesson at the same time. In 1991, Wilson increased taxes in response to a budget deficit. Years 2 and 3 of that rate increase actually resulted "in a revenue drop of $2 billion."[69] In total, it was a failed policy that played a considerable role in Republicans' poor showings in California for years to come.

---

[69] "California's Tax Follies, States Can't Tax Their Way Back to Prosperity" by Lawrence J. McQuillan and Andrew M. Gloger, published in National Review Online, http://www.nationalreview.com/nrof_comment/comment-mcquillan040703.asp

So it is little wonder why the Bush budget deficit *increased* after the tax rate increases - as opposed to decreasing. In more glib than economic terms, long ago Winston Churchill capsulated the lesson which Republicans should have known by the early 1990s when he said:

"We contend that for a nation to try to tax itself into prosperity is like a man standing in a bucket and trying to lift himself up by the handle."

As 1992 wore on and Bush 41 looked at his watch,[70] it became entirely clear that he had no intention of igniting the American spirit nor jump-starting the economy by cutting taxes. The words and actions of Kennedy and Reagan had no effect on President Bush. Rather than being bold like them, Bush acted like the cautious Eisenhower who spoke of affordable tax cuts in the midst of a recession.

Although Bush was seemingly unmoved, the strategic effect on the Republican Party was real. By changing his mind and by abandoning pro-growth policies, Bush 41 blurred the lines between Republicans and Democrats. Republican economic policies were, once again, just like the policies of the Democrats.

---

[70] President Bush, in a debate with Clinton, famously looked at his watch and was chastised by the press for being disconnected and aloof.

Bush's failure to heed Kennedy and Reagan's advice – the choice to abandon tax cuts, a critical Pillar of **The New Conservative Paradigm**, was the single largest reason President Bush lost that Fall to Bill Clinton – a candidate who campaigned by promising *a tax cut.*[71]

The careful observer will note that the presence of Ross Perot in the race was a major factor in Bush's loss as well. Perot garnered 19% of the vote - the majority of which many analysts believe would have gone to President Bush who lost to Clinton 43% to 38%.[72]

However, Perot was not much more than a single-issue champion of deficit reduction brought on by out-of-control Washington spending. As such, the Perot factor was a symptom of the Bush's problem - not its cause. Further, Bush obviously did not learn the Reagan lesson on the philosophical importance of tax cuts. He abandoned the individual and the family and sided with the need to feed government. That played no small role in his loss.

Moreover, if Bush had not raised taxes but instead cut them, and had he insisted on reduction in spending – in short, had Bush led - the deficit would not have grown and probably

---

[71] Clinton's tax cut was designed for the "Middle Class" as opposed to a true pro-growth cut. Nevertheless, in the face of Bush's tax increase, the Republicans were without Reagan's signature economic argument.

[72] Special Prosecutor Lawrence Walsh's decision to indict Casper Weinberger just days before the election also played a role and, according to some, stalled a late comeback by President Bush.

would have diminished. So, in a very real way, Bush's failures made Perot relevant. Further, recall that Bush had a 89% approval rating 18 months before the election. As liberal pundit Mark Shields said, he was "a colossus astride the political landscape." So much so that prominent Democrats declined to enter the Democrat primaries assuming Bush wasn't beatable. But as *History* witnessed, rather than unshackle the American Spirit, Bush placated government. In doing so, he became beatable and he gave his enemies the weapons with which to defeat him – tax increases.

The moral of Bush's story, therefore, was that Bush 41's weakness and abandoned promise gave rise to Perot and Clinton's victory, not the other way around. The enduring question of Republican politics everywhere is whether they will do the same again; whether they will follow Kennedy and Reagan to victory or Bush 41 (and Hoover) to defeat. *It need not be much more complicated than that*.

Clinton Bails out the Republican Party

If Bush 41 stumbled over tax cuts, the new fault line of national politics, Bill Clinton came to the rescue of Republicans. His assists to Republicans in taking back Congress were numerous and varied. Before we get to that important moment in *History*, it is worthy to note that there were certainly more prominent national Democrats available to run for president in late 1991 early 1992. The Democrats boasted such presidential campaign veterans as Richard Gephardt, Joe Biden, Al Gore, and even the venerable Ted Kennedy. All deferred to lesser-knowns, however, because of Bush 41's 1991 high approval ratings in the afterglow of the first Iraq War. Those lesser-knowns included Paul Tsongas and a little known Governor from Arkansas, Bill Clinton. Despite a much talked about victory in New Hampshire, Paul Tsongas was not able to hold off the "Comeback Kid" Bill Clinton who we all know went on to become the Democrats' nominee.

In many ways, Clinton was the opposite of his general election opponent Bush 41. Clinton was young, energetic and telegenic. As it turned out, he also campaigned somewhat the opposite of the Democrat nominees that had gone before him. Clinton made that clear when he snubbed his party elders in a revealing speech to the Wharton School of Business at the University of Pennsylvania, in Philadelphia, on April 16, 1992.

What was revealing was that Clinton had no intention of making the same mistakes as Mondale and Dukakis before him. Both had gone down in resounding defeats. For Clinton, there had to be another way, a New Democrat Way.

According to Clinton:

"If the Republicans' failed experiment in supply-side economics didn't produce growth, create upward mobility, or prepare millions of Americans to compete and win in the world economy, neither will the old Democratic theory that says we can just tax and spend our way out of any problem we face."

Beyond the rhetoric of false accusations against President Reagan,[73] Clinton clearly spoke against the orthodoxy of his party by quoting the oft-used Republican term about Democrats, i.e. that they "tax and spend."[74] Beyond speaking about it, Clinton became the first major Democrat nominee for president to make tax cuts a centerpiece of his candidacy. As of the 1992 General election, it would appear that Clinton understood Kennedy's and Reagan's lesson - *sort of.*

Rather than supply-side cuts, Clinton's tax relief took the form of "targeted" tax cuts and included:

- An investment tax credit and a new enterprise tax cut which Clinton claimed were "better than a capital gains tax cut because they reward investment in jobs, goods, and services."

- Making the research and development tax credit permanent

- A "Middle Class" tax cut

---

[73] Reagan's supply-side growth produced 92 straight months of economic growth.

[74] By speaking critically of the Republicans and the Democrats, Clinton was striking the early chords of his method of leadership, triangulation.

History knows what became of those campaign promises but as a campaign tool it was a remarkable reversal. The Democrat Clinton campaigned for tax cuts (on behalf of Americans) while the Republican Bush had to answer for his tax increases (on behalf of the government).

Less than a year after taking office, however, Bill Clinton abandoned his tax cut pledges and signed the largest tax increase in US History. Although the Major Media did not make Clinton pay for that flip-flop in the same way it did Bush 41, the Democrats in Congress certainly suffered in the very next election.

1994: The Democrats' Waterloo

Despite his claims to be a New Democrat, time would demonstrate that Bill Clinton was indeed an old tax and spend Democrat – a manager of government.

Initially, there were hints that Clinton would be a *New Democrat*. After all, it was certainly true that in March of 1993, Clinton had his Vice President Al Gore head up an initiative entitled the National Performance Review, which was not totally unlike Reagan's Grace Commission. Gore's charter was to "reinvent" and streamline government. It was also true that Clinton sided against the American labor unions on December 8, 1993 by signing the North American Free Trade Agreement and thereby creating the largest free trade zone in the World. Thus, it could be argued that Clinton initially gave hints he intended to be a reformer.

On the other hand, Clinton oversaw the adding of approximately 200,000 pages to the Code of Federal Regulations during his first three years in office (and nearly 30,000 in the last 90 days of his presidency) – nearly reversing the efforts of Reagan and matching the negative efforts of Carter. That *Old Democrat* policy was only outdone by Clinton's act of raising taxes.

At the time Clinton proposed his tax increase, the Democrats held a lead of 258 seats to 176 seats in the House of Representatives. In the Senate, the Democrats held a 57 – 43 seat advantage. Perhaps learning from the mistake of Bush 41, remarkably and tellingly, not a single Republican in either chamber of Congress voted for the Clinton tax increase.[75]

The combination of the Republicans opposition to the Clinton defense cuts, along with Clinton's Big Government health care initiative, Clinton's promotion of less than traditional values and the emerging Clinton scandals,[76] meant that in 1994 the political parties were back to the same positions they had been at the end of Reagan's term.

---

[75] Grover Norquist deserves considerable credit as well for his No New Tax Pledge efforts.

[76] Clinton's first headline-grabbing act related to gays in the military.

The Republicans once again stood for ***The New Conservative Paradigm***:

- Pro- Growth policies including opposing taxes
- Strong defense
- American Ideals and Values

The Democrats, on the other hand, once again stood for:

- Raising taxes
- A weaker defense
- Attacking America's traditional values

To reinforce those differences, and in an effort to stand *for something*, not simply *against the incumbent party*, the Republican brain trust in the House (including Newt Gingrich and Dick Armey among others) along with the help of Republican pollster Frank Luntz, another *New Conservative*, in a fit of strategic brilliance, championed the Contract with America. The *Contract with America*, a challenge of sorts, contained a variety of tax cuts, including capital gains cuts and indexation, a $500 per child tax credit, and marriage tax penalty relief.

On the traditions and values front, among other items, it sought (a) to discourage illegitimacy and teen pregnancy by prohibiting welfare to mothers under 18 years of age, and (b) to deny increased AFDC for additional children while on welfare, and (c) to enact what would be called "two-years-and-out provisions" which required work in exchange for benefits.

All in all, the *Contract with America* was a marvelous political marketing tool that clearly delineated the difference between the parties and gave voters a compelling reason to vote the majority Democrats out of power. It also marked the first time in American History that a Party's Congressional candidates ran on a unified platform. The results of election night November 8, 1994 would indeed be the Democrats' Waterloo. The Republicans gained control of both chambers of Congress, the House and the Senate for the first time in forty years – since Eisenhower championed affordable tax cuts and, in doing so, turned Republicans out into the political wilderness.

In short, the Republicans were now ahead on the three Pillars of *The New Conservative Paradigm*. More significantly, the Republican Party had completed its comeback from its depths – when the Democrats were identified (1) as the party of tax cuts, (2) as strong on defense, and (3) as the safeguard of families.

As the charts on the next page demonstrate, statistically, the reversal and its effects are difficult to challenge.

The House of Representatives and
The Senate from 1953 to 2005

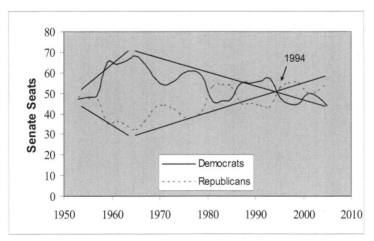

Our story does not end there, however. Indeed, the balance of the Clinton presidency and the start of the Bush 43 presidency would only serve to solidify *The New Conservative Paradigm*.

Chapter 7

Strengthening the Paradigm 1994 to 2004

"Constant repetition carries conviction."
Robert Collier

As we have seen, the Congressional Elections of 1994 were the culmination of a political reversal first begun under Ronald Reagan. Republicans took pride in their new found status and knew it could not have happened without Reagan's leadership. The Democrat leadership, on the other hand, had trouble accepting that there was a reversal and few understood then (or even now) that it happened with their help. In fact, in the 12 years between 1994 and 2006, the leaders of the Democrat Party, with few notable exceptions, were in denial as to the cause of their fate - criticizing Republican leaders as not smart[77] and voters as ill-informed – rather than truly assessing their own actions.

It would not seem to be a difficult task for a political party, in the position the Democrats were in the late 1990s, to look back to the last time they had an overwhelming majority in Congress, 1965 – and then assess the positions they held at the time and reinvigorate their party by reviving those policies. The story of the remainder of the Clinton presidency, and Bush 43's first term, however, was not that story. To the contrary, the beliefs of each party in their positions on the Pillars of *The New Conservative Paradigm* appeared to have deepened - and with them – so too the Republican majority in Congress.

In looking at these next set of charts, covering from the time Clinton was elected to Bush 43's re-election, note both the trend line and the increase since 2000 in what was the Republican majority until 2006 in Congress.

---

[77] The Democrat National Committee Chairman Howard Dean took such rhetoric to a new level by describing Republicans and/or their leaders as "brain dead," "evil," "corrupt" and "liars."

The US House of Representatives

The US Senate

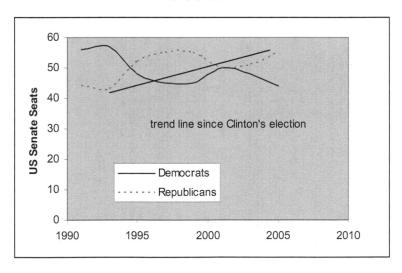

Why the New Conservative Paradigm Deepened
Pillar Number One: The Tax Side of Pro-Growth Policies

Why did the Paradigm deepen? For starters, under President Clinton "individual income taxes (excluding Social Security) . . . climbed from 7.8% of GDP to more than 10%. That marked **the highest rate in U.S. history.**"[78] How dramatic a rise was that? "Following the Reagan tax cuts of the early 1980s, federal income taxes paid by individuals in fiscal 1984 fell to 7.8% of GDP and then stayed within a relatively narrow range of approximately 7.6% to 8.5% of GDP until the 1993 [Clinton] tax hike."[79] So much for freedom and property rights – Clinton, in dramatic fashion, sided with government over the individual.

As you consider that dramatic increase in taxes since 1993, remember:

- Not one Republican in Congress voted for the 1993 Clinton tax increase – or any income tax increase since.

- In September 1999, President Clinton vetoed a $792 billion tax cut over 10 years that the Republican Congress sent to him as a pre-election year ploy. Al

---

[78] "Clinton's Untenable Taxation I, The Serious Economic Problem of the 1993 Tax Increase" by William P. Kucewicz, http://www.nationalreview.com/nrof_kucewicz/kucewicz103001.shtml

[79] Id.

Gore, the Democrats' nominee-in-waiting, previewed his 2000 campaign language by denouncing the GOP gambit as a "risky scheme."[80]

- Those higher tax rates were largely responsible for the recession that got under way during Clinton's last year and spilled over into Bush's first term.[81]

In contrast to Clinton's tax increases, President George W. Bush passed four tax cuts in his first term. On its face, that alone cemented the Republicans lead in **Pillar Number One**, Pro Growth tax cuts. *But something more, just under the surface had occurred – and it presents a strong lesson for Republicans today.*

~ ~ ~

The first Bush tax cut was signed on June 7, 2001. According to PBS:

"While the bill got significant Democratic support, *most Democrat leaders criticized it as far too large to meet other national priorities*, such as increased spending on

---

[80]http://www.americanpresident.org/history/bushgeorgew/biography/do mesticaffairs.common.shtml

[81] The Clinton recession began in the 3rd quarter of 2000 – a predictable result given the highest tax burden in US history. It is also important to note that recession started before President Bush was elected. See the "Last Economic Recession Began Under Clinton, Despite Rewrites by The Left" by Don Luskin (May 17, 2004). http://www.capmag.com/article.asp?ID=3691.

education and a Medicare prescription drug benefit, and said it would *cost* at least $4 trillion in the second decade."[82]

Bush's second tax cut came in 2002 and met with similar disdain from Democrats. Hillary Clinton questioned whether the 2002 tax cut was appropriate when, in response to Bush 43's 2002 State of the Union address, she stated: "We'll have a better idea of the ramifications of what we've heard tonight, when we *match it to the budget.*"

Not to be outdone, Democrat Senate Leader Tom Daschle stated:

> "We can't go back to deficit spending. *The tax cut must be affordable* and responsible."

Howard Dean, Democrat presidential aspirant, captured their spirit in full, however, when he said during a 2003 primary debate:

> *"We cannot afford all of the tax cuts*, [all the programs we want], and balancing the budget. Let's call this one right. Let's be fiscally responsible and balance the budget.

---

[82] http://www.pbs.org/newshour/updates/june01/tax_6-7.html
Democratic Senate Leader Tom Daschle was among those with "fiscal" objections. See "Demagoguing the President's Tax Cuts" by Joseph Perkins, http://www.signonsandiego.com/news/op-ed/perkins/20020111-9999_1e11perkins.html

In April of 2005, Hillary chimed in once again and said:

> "[W]e're getting tax cuts that we don't need and ***America cannot afford***."

After reading those quotes, ask yourself who those Democrats sound more like?

Eisenhower of the three recessions:

> "We cannot ***afford*** to reduce taxes, reduce income until we have in sight a program of expenditure that shows that the factors of income and outgo will be balanced."

Kennedy of three years of soaring revenues:

> "I repeat: our practical choice is not between a tax-cut deficit and budgetary surplus. It is between two kinds of deficits: a chronic deficit of inertia, as the unwanted result of inadequate revenues and a restricted economy; or a temporary deficit of transition, resulting from a *tax cut designed to boost the economy, increase tax revenues*, and achieve--and I believe this can be done--a budget surplus."

In truth, it is inescapable but to conclude that the Democrat leaders adopted, wholesale, Eisenhower's notion that tax cuts must be ***affordable*** – the mantra of a Minority Party that produced 40 years of Republican wilderness in Congress. To press the point, even Al Gore, who called the Bush tax cuts a "risky scheme" appeared to be channeling Barry Goldwater's 1964 criticism of the Kennedy tax cuts as "gimmickry."

It is also fair to say that the Democrats and Republicans truly had reversed positions from the time of Kennedy and Goldwater to Clinton and Bush. The Democrats during the Clinton years sided with government and the Republicans sided with individuals and families. As a result, by the first term of George W. Bush the Parties' respective positions were solidified on the first Pillar of *The New Conservative Paradigm*, pro-freedom *tax cuts* – the new fault line of American politics.

It should be no wonder then, how the Republicans increased their majority in Congress during that period of time.[83]

---

[83] Thoughtful observers will point out that despite his tax increases, Clinton was re-elected. While that is true, the problem with that observation is that the Republicans nominated Senator Bob Dole as their candidate in 1996. During his decades of service, Sen. Dole was against the Kennedy tax cuts and, as a Republican leader, shepherded through tax increases in the Senate. Simply stated, Dole was not a convincing voice for tax cuts. Even though Dole eventually came out for a tax cut, he previously refused to take the "No New Tax Pledge" and was battered by Pat Buchanan in the Republican primary for that refusal. When he did come out for a tax cut, it was a belated effort and made in earnest only after Clinton had "defined" Dole through early and relentless advertising. As a result, there simply was not any convincing definition between the candidates as there could have been – even after the nomination of Jack Kemp for vice president.

Pillar Number One: Reform Side of Pro-Growth Policies

It was Bill Clinton who announced that the era of Big Government was over. Unfortunately, neither he nor Bush 43 ended the era of spending increases.[84] Bush, however, sought to pick up the mantle of reform last brandished by President Reagan. At the outset of his first term, Bush 43 was able to pass an Education Reform Bill that sought accountability from our education establishment. His next achievement was a Tax Reform Bill that was eventually accelerated and produced a recovery out of the ashes of 9/11 and the Clinton recession. Bush then pushed for complete tax reform by naming a tax reform panel headed by former Sen. Connie Mack and signed into law bankruptcy reform.

Bush continued his reform efforts by pushing for government management initiatives such as competitive sourcing. He also sought reform in the manner in which the government cares for people in the form of his Faith Based Initiative – a reform that strengthened his commitment to **Pillar Number Three**. Bush also sought or achieved degrees of legal

---

[84] FY 1993 spending under Clinton was $1.4 trillion, $1.46 trillion in '94, $1.51 trillion in '95, $1.56 trillion in '96, $1.6 trillion in '97, $1.65 in '98, $1.7 trillion in '99 and $1.8 trillion in '00. Under Bush 41, the increases accelerated to $1.86 trillion in '01, $2.0 trillion in '02, $2.16 trillion in '03, $2.3 trillion in '04, $2.48 trillion in '05, $2.6 trillion in '06 and $2.9 trillion in '07.

reform, medical liability reform and the mother of all domestic reforms – Social Security reform.

Beyond those reforms, in what appeared at the time to be as a stroke of genius at the outset of his second term, Bush was able to cast his foreign policy in *reform* terms. No longer a policy just to root out al Qaeda, Bush's policy became a policy to *reform* oppressive governments and spread democracy throughout the World. Thusly, Bush cast his presidency as a reformist presidency domestically and internationally.

The Republican message of reform, however, was not limited to President Bush. In California, in the wake of the failed policies of the legislature and Governor Davis – policies which brought the state to the brink of bankruptcy – Californians reformed the State by recalling the Democrat Governor and replacing him with a Republican Governor who promised to take reform to a new level by "blowing-up" the old boxes of the government apparatus. Thereafter, Governor Schwarzenegger made reform his priority by passing budget reforms, workers' compensation reform, and regulatory reforms. In 2005, he made redistricting reform, pension reform and education reform national topics.

The response by the Democrat leadership to all of those Reforms was and is a predictable *NO*. In 2005, despite the passage of months, the national Democrats refused to provide a single constructive alternative reform to President Bush's Social Security Reform initiative other than raising taxes.   In California, the leadership of the Democrat Party responded with even less – they offered no meaningful reforms.[85]

As 2005 drew to a close, it was more than evident that the Republican Party was able to cast itself as the Reform Party and the Democrats as the defenders of Big Government – a moniker that is perhaps worse than the *Party of No* and clearly out of step with the times.   It is also ironic given that the Democrats have adopted the use of the word "progressive" to describe their party.   Simply stated, a party cannot be for progress when in practice it does no more than defend existing – failing – government programs.

Pillar Number Two: Protectors of the Homeland

If we start with the proposition that Americans, in 1992, trusted the Republican Party more than the Democrats on the issue of which party believed in America's purpose and protecting our homeland, then the events of the remainder of the 1990s did little to change that view.

---

[85]   Facing rigorous opposition to those reforms and a $100 million smear campaign against Arnold Schwarzenegger, those 2005 reforms did not pass. However, Arnold Schwarzenegger won a resounding reelection victory in 2006, by promising to hold the line on new taxes against an old-line Democrat, Phil Angelides, who promised to raise taxes.

Indeed, when considering the defense of America, from the outset of the Clinton administration, it was apparent to many that Clinton and the Democrats were "raiding the defense budget to fund new social spending."[86] According to a Republican backbencher, Congressman Joel Healy of Colorado, not the most partisan of the bunch:

> "Under the Clinton defense blueprint, by 1999 the defense budget will account for only 2.8 percent of gross domestic product. At no time since before World War II have we dropped below 4.4 percent of gross domestic product . . .
>
> During the same time, domestic spending is slated to increase by 12 percent, entitlements by 38 percent. What effect does this have on our military? Although only 10 percent of the Clinton defense cuts have been made, enlistment in the Armed Forces is down. The quality of recruits is dropping. The voluntary military concept which has worked so well in this country is threatened."[87]

A year later, the liberal press in the form of the New York Times upped the ante by stating that: "production of new tanks, planes, and ships can be put off for a decade or more" in support of their claim that the Clinton defense cuts did not go

---

[86] Floor speech of Joel Healy, July 19, 1994, http://thomas.loc.gov/cgi-bin/query/z?r103:H19JY4-7:

[87] Id.

far enough. The Washington Post joined in by claiming the cuts represented "incrementalism."[88]

In actual numbers, Clinton's defense budgets did indeed provide real cuts to our military budget. To be fair, Bush 41 started the reductions as part of the "peace dividend" from the end of the Cold War. The problem for the Democrats, however, was that Clinton, whose presidency had no strong foreign policy successes that could compete with the successes of Bush 41 or Reagan, *noticeably increased* the reduction from those offered by Bush 41.

As such, since the Democrats were behind on the issue to begin with – and by a significant margin - the additional cuts only served to reinforce the existing view of the Democrats. Additional reinforcement occurred when the savings that were anticipated from the dividend were spent on domestic programs - making Clinton a *tax and spend* Democrat in the grand tradition of his party.

Far worse than those cuts, however, was the fact that the Clinton policies, over time, proved to be weak and, as seminal author Richard Miniter wrote, "unleashed global terror."[89]

---

[88] "The Destruction of National Defense" by   John T. Correll, http://www.afa.org/magazine/1993/05edit93.asp

[89] *Losing bin Laden: How Bill Clinton's failures Unleashed Global Terror* by Richard Miniter

Clinton's False Sense of Security

For those not paying close attention to the Clinton era defense policies, frankly, his policies did not appear clearly damaging to the United States. Clinton's assist in Northern Ireland resulted in an opening to the long-standing divisions in the area. Clinton's bombing of Bosnia appeared to end a conflict via an air war. Clinton "showed" that America was interested in Middle East peace by attempting to broker a grand deal to which Yasser Arafat simply would not take yes for an answer. Thus, many a casual observer claimed that the US was at peace.

Many less than casual observers on the Left also came to that erroneous conclusion - if not peddled that false sense of security. Chief among them was Hillary Clinton who claimed that Bill Clinton "gave us eight years of peace" during her 2004 Democrat Convention Speech delivered to like-minded delegates. Time, however, has made it quite clear that that was not the case.

Glimpses that turned to glare of Clinton's weak foreign policy surfaced during his presidency in the form of:

- Clinton's failure to respond with much more than a police investigation to the 1993 al Qaeda bombings of the Twin Towers – 8 years before they were brought down within months of the end of Clinton's presidency

– the planning of which occurred largely during Clinton's presidency.

- Clinton's "destruction of an empty building in central Baghdad" in response to Saddam Hussein's assassination plot against Bush 41.[90]

- Clinton's failure to truly hold Hussein accountable – with other than bombing raids - despite countless UN resolutions and his countless violations.

Perhaps, at least in retrospect, the worst action taken by Clinton was the ignominious withdrawal of America troops from Somalia after the downing of a Blackhawk helicopter. That battle became a Hollywood movie and more importantly, the withdrawal engendered the following response from Osama bin Laden:

"Our boys went to Somalia and prepared themselves carefully for a long war . . . Our boys were shocked by the low morale of the American soldier, and they realized that the American soldier was just a paper tiger. He was unable to endure the strikes that were dealt to his army, so he fled, and America had to stop all its bragging."

After reading that, can there be any doubt whatsoever that bin Laden believed that leadership under Bill Clinton was not the same leadership that induced Iran to release the American hostages on the eve of the Reagan presidency?

---

[90] Id. at 55.

Can there be any doubt that the meager responses by the Clinton administration to the 1st al Qaeda attack on the Twin Towers - and the 7 others during the Clinton years against US interests – convinced bin Laden that he could plan and get away with flying planes into the Twin Towers?[91] Only the most ardent partisan could think otherwise and, in time, most of Americans would see that as well.

As a result, America closed the Clinton years with a clear understanding that the Republicans maintained a clear edge on **Pillar Number Two**, *Belief in America and its defens*e.

The early success of George W. Bush in continuing to reinforce Americans' view of which party was ahead on the Second Pillar can be summed up in two words: "Security Moms."   The designation was part of the never-ending desire on the part of the Media and consultants to market the latest "swing" voter group which the national parties were required to court. If you recall, the 1990s saw the rise of the "Soccer Moms."   For them, the parties were told that they had to address their concerns on such "kitchen table" issues as

---

[91] The al Qaeda attacks/plots included: (1) the December 1992 Aden Hotel attacks in Yemen, (2) 1993- car bomb attack on New York's Twin Towers, (3) 1993- attacks in Somalia including the downing of a Blackhawk helicopter, (4) 1995- al Qaeda plan to bomb multiple US planes code named "Project Bojinka" discovered, (5) al Qaeda bombs US interests in Riyadh, Saudi Arabia, (6) 1998- near simultaneous bombings by al Qaeda of US embassies in Nairobi & Dar es Salaam killing 200 and injuring 4500, (7) 2000- failed attack on the USS Sullivan in Yemen discovered.

education and childcare.   As the first post 9/11 presidential election in 2004 drew near, however, the "Soccer Mom" designation gave way to "Security Moms."

The Bush administration's response to 9/11 was nothing if not comprehensive. It included a war in Afghanistan to replace an ugly, brutal regime that harbored, if not sponsored, Osama bin Laden and al Qaeda. It included the Patriot Act and the Department of Homeland Security.[92] It has included countless efforts to win the War on Terror – efforts that were chronicled by Richard Miniter, a *New Conservative,* in his book *Shadow War*, *The Untold Story of How America is Winning the War on Terror* – his follow up best seller to his first best seller, *Losing bin Laden*. And, of course, it included removing Saddam Hussein from Iraq in contrast to Clinton's bombing of Iraq.

All the while, there can be little doubt that leading Democrats fought the Bush administration's efforts. Some blamed US policy for 9/11 in the latest manifestation of the "Blame America First" crowd. Others claimed that a war in Afghanistan was unwinnable and we would be bogged down in the mountain winters of that region.   Before the Iraq War started, the Left claimed that the war would result in hundreds of thousands of deaths. After the war began, and despite US

---

[92] Democrats may rightly claim that President Bush resisted the Department of Homeland Security at first. Nevertheless, he came to champion it and will get the credit, or perhaps the blame, just as Clinton claims credit for welfare reform – which was a Republican/Contract with America idea.

tanks rolling into Baghdad, the Left claimed that we were losing the war. As for Iraqi elections, they too were claimed not to be possible. Countless Democrats decried our break with France, Germany and Russia on the issue and, perhaps in response, they ran a presidential candidate in 2004 – John Kerry - who was an "internationalist."

Few on the Left backtracked, however, even after revelations of the French and Russian Iraqi bribes (which explained their opposition to the wars). Nor did the incredible success of the Afghani and Iraqi elections have any effect. Instead, the Left could be seen pounding away at America and its Purpose in the World - all the while ignoring the misdeeds of those fighting against the US. Although American impatience with the war was beginning to show in 2005, the Democrats were reinforcing their weak security credentials leaving the Republicans firmly ahead on **Pillar Number Two**.

Pillar Number Three:
Respect for American Traditions and Values

It would appear beyond the point of argument that the Clinton years reinforced the divide between the parties on the 3rd Pillar of *The New Conservative Paradigm*, respect for traditions and values. Indeed, for most of the Nation, including many Democrats, the Clinton years were a bit too much for the senses.

Although Clinton enjoyed a certain status as a Southern Governor replete with Baptist ties - a factor that helped him in his election over the irreligious Dole - who can forget that Clinton's first high profile act was an initiative seeking social change: Clinton's Gays in the Military program?[93]   It was undertaken within days after his inauguration and did not get "resolved" until July of that year – and wound up satisfying very few when the "Don't Ask, Don't Tell Policy" was adopted.   Thereafter, the Nation was entreated to the sordid details of Jennifer Flowers, Paula Jones and, of course, Monica Lewinsky.   Combined with Whitewater, the fundraising scandals and ultimately Impeachment, for many people in the Country, there was a perceived risk that turning on the television might not be in their child's best interest.

Beyond the Clinton chronicles, if the 1980s saw the zenith of the Religious Right's influence on Republican politics, the 1990s saw the rise of the far Left's influence on, if not control of, the Democrat Party.   Their agenda seemed to accelerate during this tumultuous period.

---

[93] Contrast that with Reagan's first high profile act which was the complete deregulation of oil and gas.

The Drive to Remove God
From the Public Square Continues

There was no easing up on the drive by the Left to change traditions and values as they related to God in the Public Square during this period. In the decade of the 1990s, examples abounded:

- In 1993, long before the 2003 Alabama case, the "Ten Commandments, despite the fact that they . . . are depicted in engraved stone in the U.S. Supreme Court" were barred from the Georgia Court House.[94]

- Also in 1993, historical classic artwork was barred from public schools because of its religious theme - this time in South Dakota.[95]
- In 1994, it was ruled unconstitutional for a school graduation ceremony to contain an opening or closing prayer.[96]

After the century turned, a new height was reached in 2002. The liberal 9th Circuit Court of Appeals ruled that the Pledge of

---

[94] *Harvey v. Cobb County* – an appeals case heard in Georgia and cited in David Barton's *Original Intent, The Courts, The Constitution & Religion.*

[95] *Washegèsic v. Bloomingdale Public Schools*, 33 F.3d 679 (6th Cir. 1994) [held that the display of a portrait of Christ, a copy of Warren Sallman's "Head of Christ," in a hallway outside the gymnasium violated the Establishment Clause] cited in *Original Intent.*

[96] *Harris v. Joint School District No. 241*, 41F.3d 447 (9th Cir. 1994). Of course, every session of Congress begins with an invocation and as we have seen, Congress requested that Washington institute a Day of Prayer on the same day they approved of the final wording of the 1st Amendment.

Allegiance was unconstitutional based on the inclusion of the phrase "Under God" – a ruling that, by its logic, necessarily would require the removal of the words "In God We Trust" from all of our currency. Even leaders of the Democrat Party had to recoil given the implications – but few doubt those implications remain the intentions of the Left.

Alternative Lifestyles and Mainstream America

The Left's social agenda in the 1990s, however, was not limited to the removal of God from the Public Square. In ways too demonstrable and troubling for the majority of Americans, the advocacy of alternative lifestyle rights appeared to move toward center stage during that time. Keep in mind for purposes of this book and as we review this history, the point of the discussion is *only* to put the issue in historical context as it affects politics at large – not to decide the issue. In that light, for many Americans, the push on social issues by the Left and their Democrat patrons has been too much and too fast and that worked against the Democrats politically.

Keep in mind that the 1990s were certainly not the first time that gay issues were brought before Americans nor the first time the Country struggled to come to grips with related issues. By the 1990s, however, the role of political parties regarding gay rights was becoming more defined. Prior to that, the parties were not always far apart on the issue. During the

1950s, the US taxpayer paid for a government report that concluded that "homosexuals . . . are not proper persons to be employed in government . . ."[97]

In the 1960s, Hollywood, not surprisingly, led in a different direction when it revised its production code to include the following language "homosexuality and other sexual aberrations may now be treated with care, discretion and restraint." In the 1970s, Hollywood productions began featuring gay life, a theme that seems to pervade many of the movies and television programs of today.

In a glimpse of things to come, the 1980 Democrat Convention featured an openly gay "candidate" for vice president (Mel Boozer) who addressed the convention. In 1984, (in where else but Berkeley), California became the first municipality to extend "spousal" benefits to domestic partners. In 1989, Congress only "censured" openly gay Mass. Rep. Barney Frank despite his permitting a homosexual prostitute to use Frank's home for his activities. That same year, the American Bar Association, home to many a trial lawyer, overwhelmingly passed a resolution seeking federal legislation in favor of rights for gays and lesbians.

---

[97] Interim Report submitted to the Committee on Expenditures in the Executive Departments by its Subcommittee on Investigations pursuant to S. Res. 280 (81st Congress).

If the 1990s were not the first decade that the issue of gay rights arose, it certainly became the decade that the courts and the legislatures of America became the forum for the gay rights issues.   US restrictions on the immigration of gays were rescinded in 1990, California Governor Pete Wilson vetoed a gay employment rights bill in 1991, the Kentucky Supreme Court struck down a sodomy law in 1992 while in the same year Colorado voters banned state and municipal rights for gays – a vote that touched off similar drives throughout the Country. In 1993, the Hawaii Supreme Court addressed the gay marriage issue in the same year the Massachusetts Senate became the first state to approve a law to protect gay students against discrimination in public schools.

Similar processes continued throughout the 1990s (and continue to this day) that included a loss by one vote of a federal law in 1996 that would have banned employment discrimination against gays and the eventual signing of the Marriage and Defense Act.   The drive had quickened to the point that, in 1997, the National Gay and Lesbian Task Force was able to boast that "Gay rights legislation at the city and county level has advanced at a dramatic pace in the 1990s" which included gay rights ordinances in 157 US cities and counties at that time.

Today, the gay movement seeks, and in many cases has achieved, not just greater anti-discrimination laws but marriage/civil union rights, parenting rights and/or the re-defining of the family unit, health care rights and curriculum changes in schools reflective of their movements.

Again, the point of raising the issue, in this book, is not to debate the merits of gay rights, nor is it to determine who is right or wrong in God's eyes – it is not even to recommend a political resolution. Indeed, like the issue of abortion, it may well be that a "resolution" of the issue is illusive. The point of raising the issue is two-fold.

First, a considerable majority of Americans disagree with that social agenda and the pace of change that is sought – a significant amount of which unwaveringly if not virulently so. Witness the rise in the number of states passing bans on same-sex-marriage.[98] Of those not against the agenda, many are libertarian to the extent that they are willing to live and let live **provided** that they are not required by government or anyone else to give up their own traditions and values.

Unlike the issue of abortion, however – and this is the crux of the matter for many - whereas someone's decision or agenda related to abortion *may* not directly affect their neighbor (your neighbor could have an abortion without your knowledge), in the view of many Americans, the Far Left's agenda *and tactics* with regard to gay rights necessarily does.

---

[98] For instance, in 2006, Tennessee voters passed a gay marriage ban 81% to 19%.

No greater example of that could be found than in the public school context where the gay agenda is pushed on children of remarkably young age. For the vast majority on the Right, that is not acceptable. For many in the middle, it is pushing too much on their children at an early age – and, the irony is not lost on a majority that the Left simultaneously demands that the community stay out of their bedrooms at the same time they seek to push their agenda into school rooms.

Of course, the same analysis holds true for the issue of God in the Public Square. For the Left, success is not defined by the tolerance they so eagerly demand of others - but, instead, by their ability to take away the traditions of others. Such hostile takeover attempts of any aspect of a culture are rarely greeted with indifference - let alone an issue so central to the very meaning of life.

Thus, it is certainly no wonder that on all those issues the so-called Religious Right has fought back seeking to hold onto the traditions and values they know and cherish. In truth, however, this coalition of those willing to hold onto their traditions and values and ideals - if for no other reason than to have their children grow up like them - without all the background noise of the modern World – is much broader than the fit of any label such as "traditional values."

As for the second reason, the issue that is most relevant to *The New Conservative Paradigm*, simply stated, Americans realize that it is the leadership of the Democrats, often referred to as the San Francisco Democrats, that supports that agenda – an agenda which runs counter to the simple life so many have known and want for their children.

So, whether in the form of their preference for the nostalgia of Reagan's "Shining City on a Hill" or the decency of President George W. Bush, contrasted with the Clinton trysts, as of 2004, the majority of Americans believed that the Republican Party was ahead on the Third Pillar of *The New Conservative Paradigm*, preserving our traditions and values. Given the hold the far Left has on the Democrat Party and their dedication to that agenda, it is a lead not likely to be lost for some time to come.

Chapter 8

Republicans Return Clinton's Favor 2004 to 2006

**"Nothing is easier than the expenditure of public money.
It doesn't appear to belong to anyone.
The temptation is overwhelming to bestow it on somebody."
Republican President Calvin Coolidge**

As we have seen, leading up to the 1994 Congressional election, the Republicans' best friend was Bill Clinton. He started off his presidency with a nod toward the Left by pushing a policy change for homosexuals serving in the military. Not long after, he broke his campaign promise of a tax cut and instead signed a massive tax increase. Republicans voted against the tax bill in unison and in doing so, gave greater meaning to the vision that Reagan laid out in the decade before. In a very real way, Clinton coalesced Republicans in a way that not even Reagan did.

Republicans followed up on their opposition to the Clinton tax hike with the Contract for America. It was the first time in Congressional history that candidates for the House of Representatives ran on a unified and specific platform. By giving the voters a clear choice, a choice that highlighted two of the three *Pillars of the New Conservative Paradigm* (Pro-Growth/Reform and Respect for Traditions and Values), Republicans took back the Congress.

Nine out of ten of the provisions of the Contract for America passed the House – and for some time thereafter, Congressional Republicans acted like reformists. In doing so, and by rejecting calls for further tax hikes, Congressional Republicans strengthened the Republicans' considerable lead on **Pillar Number One**: *Pro-growth Policies and Reform* and renewed their commitment to **Pillar Number Three**: *Respect for American Traditions and Values.*

From 2004 to 2006, once again, *things changed.* The 24 hours news cycle/Internet age had taken hold in earnest. In the competition for ratings, the Media and websites exaggerate events and those exaggerations, in turn, foster exaggerated responses from politicians – most often in the form of new government programs or spending to "solve" each and every perceived inequity. That dynamic is, of course, a dangerous and near irresistible invitation to become a proponent of government – and it is an especially bad temptation given that we are more than a quarter century since Reagan aptly stated, "The nine most terrifying words in the English language are 'I'm from the government and I'm here to help.'"

It is against that backdrop that we can view how, shortly after Bush's re-election in 2004, the Republican leaders began to return Clinton's favor. The obvious change between the Republican leaders from 1994 and the Republican leaders of the 2005/2006 Congress manifested itself for all to see in 2005. By many accounts, 2005 became the year of spending. The 2005 federal transportation bill was a monument to pork barrel spending. It featured a mega, mega-million-dollar-bridge, in Alaska, to serve a virtually uninhabited island – aptly referred to as the *Bridge to Nowhere*.

The Republican leadership reached a rhetorical low in September of 2005. House Majority Leader, Republican Tom Delay, who helped Republicans and the reform movement in the 1990s declared an "ongoing victory" against fat in the US budget. Incredibly, he claimed that there was no fat left to cut in the federal budget. He concluded his dispiriting thoughts by stating that "After 11 years of Republican majority we've pared [the budget] down pretty good."   Conservatives everywhere, Independents in many places and even Democrats, could not take his comment seriously – although the transformation of Republican leadership would have serious effects.

Then, in response to Hurricane Katrina, in October of 2005, the Republican Congress passed an aid package that, in all likelihood, will end up larger, in gross dollars, than the entire 1970 federal budget - which was roughly $190 billion dollars.

Through it all, President Bush did not blemish his record of failing to impose a single veto.   According to **New Conservative** Mona Charen, "The Republican Congress …increased spending by 33 percent since George W. Bush took office" and "Inflation-adjusted spending on the combined budgets of the 101 largest programs Republicans vowed to eliminate in 1995 has grown by 27 percent." After all was said and done, in October of 2005, Congressional approval ratings sank to depressing lows – reflecting the fact that there is no majority in this Country that approves of monumental spending.

In 2006, the Congressional Republicans did – well – nothing particularly good that was visible. Instead, they kept spending for which there is no majority constituency. There also is no question that Hastert, Frist - and Bush by extension - wanted to do nothing more than run out the clock in '06. They were, in effect, looking over their shoulders instead of forging ahead. There was no evident vision and no plan – let alone good communication. But that was not for a lack of ideas or problems to fix. It was a lack of leadership.

Indeed, despite the impending expiration of the Bush tax cuts – and despite the fact that the Country has no appetite for tax increases – and despite the fact that tax cuts had been the one common winning issue for the previous 7 presidential contenders, the renewal of the tax cuts was barely mentioned let alone made a center piece of the 2006 election.

As for reform, that didn't happen either – and there were plenty of opportunities. Immigration? The answer is fairly obvious. Congress discussed it and in the end came up with almost nothing. Social Security and Medicare? The answer is fairly obvious as well. They discussed it and in the end came up with exactly nothing.

All of this is to say that by November of 2006, the Republican leadership was offering voters little in the way of a vision for the future, no identifiable plan and nothing to achieve. *Instead of staying ahead, they allowed themselves to be caught.*

It certainly did not have to be so. After all, the Democrat leaders still did not offer much in the form of a positive agenda – no Contract with America, no 100 Day Plan, not much more than they had in previous years when they earned the moniker of the ***Party of No***. Indeed, rather than offering a plan, their party leaders seemed to go into hiding down the stretch: Pelosi, Reid, Murtha, Durbin, Dodd, Kennedy and the like were *Missing In Action*.

In politics, they say you can't beat something with nothing. That axiom applied well as to how the Republicans gained an advantage over the Democrats from 1980 forward. Throughout 2005 and 2006, however, the Republicans were offering little more than nothing.

After the 2006 election, many a pundit argued that the Iraq War cost the Republicans the 2006 election. While it is true that the ongoing war did not help Republican Congressional candidates, it was not the central reason they lost.

You see, in politics, if you are not moving forward, it's easy to get knocked off your perch. When leaders are not cutting new paths and when they are not doing what it takes to stay ahead, they become subject to the vagaries of circumstances. Put another way, when someone is only treading water, even a small wave can overtake them.

2006 featured the Iraq War, Global Warming, and the Foley Congressional page scandal – none of those issues were so large as to cause the November defeats – especially considering (a) that the loss of American lives in Iraq (heartbreaking in any amount) is dwarfed by losses from prior major wars, (b) that Bush had a robust economy, (c) that Bush had a great judicial record (as far as objective conservatives were concerned), and

(d) considering the worthy foreign policy goal of defeating terrorism.

BUT. When a party is perceived as doing nothing, the other party, the Media and circumstances define that party instead of that party defining themself. In other words, the Foley page scandal became a big story when Congressional Republicans had no compelling story of their own to tell or when the president failed to tell the one he had. So it can be no surprise that when voters came out of the booth to answer exit polls on November 7th, 2006, of course Iraq and Foley were the only questions to be asked. Why shouldn't it be? - Republicans never gave them an alternate storyline.

Simply stated, the Republican Congress looked weak because it was not leading. Bush suffered because he allowed them not to lead and, in effect, he was not leading. Combine that with Media distortions and the 6-year itch and you have your recipe for mid-term losses – not huge losses (in 1994 the Democrats lost more) because the Democrats were still not offering anything – but losses nonetheless.

When all was said and done, by November of 2006, the Republicans forfeited their lead on **Pillar Number One**, *Pro-Growth policies/reforms*. They issued no challenge to the American people and had stopped acting like reformists and failed to pursue tax cuts. In response to the breach of the ongoing Contract with America, Republican voters, who are far more demanding of their party and its candidates than Democrat voters, were disenchanted. Independent voters were put off by the Iraq War - especially in light of the lack of an alternative storyline - and the Democrats, despite offering no plan of their own, won back the Congress in 2006 by default.

Chapter 9

Republicans Continue Their Losing Streak

The Election of 2008

"Winning is habit. Unfortunately, so is losing."
Vince Lombardi

In the end, the 2008 presidential election would be known as an election of "firsts." Those firsts included the first Black president, the first woman from a major party with a chance to get the nomination (Hillary Clinton), the first woman Republican vice presidential nominee (Sarah Palin) and the first time two Senators squared off for the presidency. It also featured the largest age differential between candidates in presidential election history and it was the first time that the social-networking aspect of the Internet would play an important role in politics.

Beyond those firsts, it was the first time, in a very long time -1928 to be exact - that neither the incumbent party's president nor its vice president sought their party's nomination. That meant that the 2008 presidential cycle had a wide-open nature to it which did not come without its long-term effects. Among them was a growing sense that politics was no longer cyclical but, instead, a constant affair. Indeed, presidential candidates began to emerge even before the 2006 Midterm elections.

After the Midterm elections, and especially towards the end of the cycle, the struggling economy and unprecedented and pressing Wall Street troubles dominated the election. Even so, amidst such gathering urgency and seemingly endless cycles, the underlying paradigm remained. Voters' *hope* for prosperity remained a dominant political force and they chose a president based, in part, on the promise of tax cuts to 95% of Americans. They also chose against a party that was believed to let economic matters get out of control - perhaps the other side to the coin of proactive reforms, i.e. failing to reform.

Today, the latest political news seemingly appears nearly everywhere. The airwaves are filled daily with political prognostications and prognosticators speak of presidential candidates almost within hours of an inauguration. The election of 2008 played a not insignificant role in that dynamic.

Even before the 2006 Midterm elections, Republicans began to emerge as potential presidential candidates all the while knowing that Vice President Cheney would not seek the nomination. Among them were the Republican Senate Leader Bill Frist and the eventual nominee, Senator John McCain. Within that rivalry, Frist was disadvantaged because he still was required, at least nominally, to stand with his sitting President George W. Bush.

McCain, on the other hand, had less such motivation and returned to his role as a media darling. Knowing that the Media would broadcast his contrarian views, McCain was all too happy to oblige by stating views inconsistent with the Republican Party line. That jockeying for position, combined with the well-deserved 2006 midterm losses for Republicans, contributed to a poor finish for the Bush Presidency and a muddled Republican brand.   The overall result was that Republicans got off to a poor start in the 2008 presidential sweepstakes.

It should be noted that the 2008 cycle was certainly not the first time that presidential politics got off to quick start - after all, Andrew Jackson began running almost immediately after a "Corrupt Bargain" cost him the presidency in 1824.[99] Coming

---

[99] In the 1824 election, Andrew Jackson obtained what was thought at the time to be a plurality of the popular vote and the most Electoral Votes. The

out of 2006 midterm losses, combined with the now ubiquitous and often biased Media, the early Republican fighting made it very difficult for Republicans to develop a cohesive narrative, let alone govern well, between 2005 and 2008. The ailing economy and 8 years of a presidency only made matters worse - and unlike the years following 1824 - the endless cycle does not appear to be leaving us.[100]

Unable to define their own compelling narrative, the 2006 to 2008 narrative that did develop was that the national Republicans were simply not that popular with the voting public. They had lost the Congress in 2006 amidst criticism from the Left and the Right on spending. Between 2006 and 2008, President Bush would suffer lagging polling numbers at the hands of an abusive Media and a deteriorating economy.

---

presence of 3 candidates in the race deprived any of the 3 from obtaining a majority of Electors – thereby throwing the election into the House of Representatives. The term "Corrupt Bargain" referred to a "deal" between then Speaker of the House Henry Clay and the eventual winner John Quincy Adams. It was said Adams promised Clay the post of Secretary of State in exchange for Clay's efforts to persuade the House to vote for Adams. Adams did win and Clay became Secretary of State. None too pleased; Jackson began running again almost immediately and became president four years later.

[100] If President Obama is re-elected, it is more than unlikely that Vice President Biden would be the presumptive nominee in 2016 if he ran at all. In other words, almost immediately after the November 2012 election, the next presidential sweepstakes would be under way on both sides and, if Obama was re-elected, his second term would be hampered by Democrats seeking to differentiate themselves from him just as Republicans did to Bush in 2005.

Unemployment had risen from 4.4% in early 2007 to above 7% by the fall of 2008. As the unemployment numbers rose on Main Street an unprecedented financial crisis hit Wall Street. The crisis would be attributed, in large part, to the Republicans and false claims related to deregulation. Thoughtful observers know that decades of bad, government housing policies distorted the market and played a central role in Wall Street's troubles - even so, while in power, Republicans failed to proactively do something about it, i.e. they failed to get out in front of the issue by sufficiently pushing the mantle of reform in the face of Democrats who resisted the necessary reforms. As a result, suffering the fate of a party in power, Republicans bore the brunt of voter anger on the economy. So intense were those feelings that more voters in May of *2011* still blamed Bush more than Obama for the bad economy of *2011*.

For the Democrats, the gathering storm of 2008 represented an easy entre to victory. Defeating an incumbent or an incumbent party is *usually* a two-step matter for the challenger (1) convincing voters, if they don't already know, that the times are so bad or the incumbent is not doing the job and (2) that the challenger has a better plan. I say "usually" because if times are so bad, sometimes that alone is enough even if the challenger offers precious little in the way of a way forward.

FDR certainly was the beneficiary of the latter in 1932. He actually campaigned against Hoover's excessive spending in route to the White House before changing his tune considerably. Times were so bad by 1932 that - along with 12 years of Republicans presidents - voters were ready for *Change* without much coaxing.

The story of the 2008 election was in part that story, but that was not all. The Republicans flat out did not nominate someone able to articulate why government had failed the voters, let alone provide voters with an inspirational path to economic recovery and achievement. To the contrary, Republicans nominated someone who openly questioned the Bush tax cuts and, who, instead of unequivocally advocating government reform, McCain went on to offer a Big Government solution to the Nation's housing crisis by stating, in a debate with Obama, that he wanted the US government to buy up all of the bad mortgages.

Why John McCain failed to do that was not much of a mystery. However honorable his service in the military, inclusive of an astonishingly heroic prisoner of war saga, McCain openly admitted that economics was not his forte. In that way, McCain was not unlike former Republican President and former General Eisenhower. McCain also shared Eisenhower's lack of a partisan bent. Indeed, McCain relished his "Maverick" status in the Media and his appeal to Independents.

Returning to McCain and economics, in 2005, in a remarkably candid comment to then Wall Street Journal editor Stephen Moore, McCain said: "I'm going to be honest: I know a lot less about economics than I do about military and foreign policy issues. *I still need to be educated.*" As he spoke around the Country during the 2008 cycle, that lack of knowledge was apparent as he failed articulate a clear vision and even proclaimed that the fundamentals of the economy were sound when Main Street knew they were not.

Amidst that self-proclaimed ignorance, McCain also said that the Bush tax cuts were "way too tilted to the rich." Our comparison to Eisenhower is now complete. McCain simply was not a voice for the power, political or economic, for tax cuts. To the contrary, despite rising tax burdens, he played right into the hands of the Democrats on the issue by echoing their divisive political class warfare instead of casting tax cuts for what they can be: an empowering economic process.

Even so, eventually McCain did offer Americans "tax cuts" in the form of targeted tax relief along with the continuation of the Bush tax cuts. However, like Bob Dole before him, McCain's career skepticism of tax cuts undercut his believability on the issue.

The sum total of McCain's performance as a candidate on the issue of the economy and tax cuts hardly inspired an increasingly uneasy electorate watching Wall Street titans fall and looking for leadership - let alone being a clarion for tax cuts like Reagan in 1980. To the contrary, McCain wound up touting Big Government solutions not a means to private, entrepreneurial success. McCain wanted to manage not lead.

For his part, candidate Obama harped on the failing economy (as did his main primary opponent Hillary Clinton) with a helping hand from the American Media. Obama's prescription to help people did include more government programs to be sure - a tried and true Democrat prescription - but that was not all. Learning from candidate Bill Clinton, candidate Obama touted tax cuts as well. But unlike Clinton they would not just be for the middle class. Obama claimed he would lower taxes for 95% of Americans. To be sure, his tax cut claims were phony but they were not effectively rebutted by the economically challenged McCain.

In the final analysis, McCain was not a credible voice for tax cuts, or the economy, and Obama likely outflanked him on the issue. Given the magnitude of the economic issues of the day, it is hard but to conclude that the prosperity issue was the main issue of the day and Obama flat out beat McCain on the issue.

Pillars 2 & 3 Get Lost in the Shuffle

So where did that leave Pillars Two & Three? Muted at best is the likely answer. Clearly, John McCain had the edge when it came to **Pillar No. 2**: *Belief in America and Her Defense*. He was a war hero contrasted with a candidate of questionable associations - including Weather Underground bomber Bill Ayers - not to mention questionable beliefs. While the Media protected Obama in many ways, including failing to delve sufficiently into his past, the fact remains that McCain's lead on Pillar Two was in no way sufficient to trump the bad economy and McCain's inability to lead on that issue.

Worse yet, the Iraq and Afghanistan Wars, whose longevity didn't help Republicans in 2006, would do no better for them in 2008. In the final analysis, 2008 was not an election that pivoted on national defense and to the extent that it had an effect, it motivated more voters on the Left than on the Right.

Pillar No. Three, *Respect for Tradition and Traditional Values,* didn't provide McCain much of a boost either – even if on paper it should have. After all, Obama's religious identity was hardly a plus in 2008. His reverend, Reverend Wright, was such a liability that Obama distanced himself before he officially got in the race. When the truth about Wright got out, it could hardly be said that Obama benefitted from those religious ties. In addition to that, many voters wondered whether Obama was Christian or Muslim based in part by his middle name: Hussein.

Further, on the face of it, Obama's ties to radicals from the past, whether it was Saul Alinsky (the radical, far Left "organizer") or Bill Ayers, just to mention a few, weren't exactly appealing to a majority of Americans. All combined that should have provided a grand opening for McCain. Opening or not, however, McCain was not able to capitalize on the issue in a meaningful way. To the contrary, McCain was reluctant to push the issue of *Respect for Tradition and Traditional Values* because it was not in his persona to do so. He had an understated demeanor on such issues and therefore was either unwilling or incapable to effectively leverage these issues to his advantage.

~ ~ ~

In retrospect, many voters on the Right will remember the 2008 election as the election that the Media, in earnest, helped a Democrat nominee by promoting him and refusing to discuss his controversial and inexperienced career. On the other hand, that same press raked the private life of Republican Sarah Palin and her family over the coals and discounted her experience almost altogether while being apologists for Obama's lack of experience.

For others, they will look closely at the numbers and know that the turnout on the Democrats' side during the primaries was dramatically higher than the Republican side. That was due, in part, because of the opportunity for Democrats to vote for the first Black president or the first female president. It was also due to the fact that Republicans voters still did not have much motivation to turnout - a problem dating back to the 2006 elections. They still were looking for a Leader of *We the People* not a manager of government. The Left, on the other hand, was flat out more motivated after eight years of a Republican Presidency.

Still others will claim that the vice presidential nominee Sarah Palin played a decisive role in the outcome of the 2008 election. As the Vice Chairman of the California Republican Party at the time, I can tell you that the Palin effect on the 2008 was both good and bad. Prior to her pick, the McCain campaign was lagging badly when it came to attracting volunteers to walk precincts, make phone calls and the like. After her pick, the number of volunteers jumped dramatically. There can be no doubt that she pumped up huge portions of the Republican base. On the other hand, Palin became a lightning rod after some of the worst treatment a candidate has ever suffered at the hands of the Media. Her choice also undercut McCain's narrative that Obama lacked experience. All in all, I can't conclude that the election outcome would have been different if McCain had picked someone else.

In the end, the failing economy was the main issue of the 2008 election. It was that bad and perhaps no Republican could have won under those circumstances. Even so, the nomination of a Republican candidate for whom prosperity was not a compelling theme seemed to fulfill Lombardi's warning that losing can become habit.

A Democrat did win and despite the Media's crowing, Obama's victory was, in fact, limited – not even reaching 53% of the voters. Further, as we have seen, Obama did not dominate all three Pillars. He lagged behind on Pillars 2 & 3 and, although he outflanked McCain on **Pillar No. 1**, that did not mean Obama was entirely convincing on the issue. Indeed, it was obvious his commitment to true tax relief, or even sensible economics, was just a campaign promise. And like Bill Clinton before him, Obama would be seen as backtracking on the issue before long. That and other issues would lay the groundwork for the 2010 midterms and historic losses for Democrats in Congress.

Chapter 10

The Democrats Out Do Their 1994 Losses & The Tea Party Emerges As a Political Force

The Election of 2010

**"The one good thing about repeating your mistakes
is that you know when to cringe"
Anonymous**

If the 2006 and 2008 Republicans were hard at work on a losing streak, the Democrats of 2008 and 2010 were not about to let them stand on the stage of errors alone. Just as they did in 1993, the 2010 Democrats would give voters plenty of reasons to turn them out and with that, for the 3rd time in 16 years, the House of Representatives changed hands after four decades of one-party rule.

The kick-off to the 2010 election cycle was nothing short of startling. In January of 2010, a relative unknown, Scott Brown, became a national figure (if not a sensation) and won the "Kennedy" Senate seat in a special election following Ted Kennedy's death. For their part, the results of the Fall 2010 election were just as historic. The Republicans gained 63 House seats – the most in any midterm election since 1938 - along with picking up 6 Senates without losing any Senate seats (a rare occurrence). The magnitude of those Democrat losses, just four years after they won the House, was a clear testament as to how quickly political winds can change in modern American politics.

~   ~   ~

The presidency of Barack Obama started out with great fanfare in 2009 .*even with his smaller than advertised victory.* Obama was the first Democrat since Jimmy Carter to win more than 50% of the vote. The American Media was ready to continue the hit parade while the Norwegian Nobel Committee nominated Obama for the Nobel Prize just one month into his presidency and ultimately gave him the prize for reasons that seemed unjustified to say the least. However auspicious the start, Obama could not sustain the promise attributed to him because Obama lacked an understanding of leadership. He had no experience in consensus building. He only had a penchant for relying on government at literally every turn - not setting rational goals for achievement. He believes in government not people.

With respect to the consensus building, politics is a game of addition – successful politics anyway. Great leaders, when faced with a divided electorate, not to mention difficult economic times, use a limited agenda to forge consensus out of broken paradigms. Once they achieve an initial success, they seek a broader consensus. In the 1980's Reagan faced a divided Republican Party and a fractured and dispirited Nation. Concentrating on the prosperity issue and our national prestige, Reagan first brought Republicans together and then Independents and even many Democrats. Indeed, so successful was Reagan at bringing people together, that in time he could rely on a group of *Reagan Democrats*. Few other presidents have had such success at building consensus let alone are able to claim a voting block from the other party in their name.

There is little doubt that Obama faced a divided electorate and a difficult economic climate when he took office. However, rather than start with a limited agenda designed to build consensus, Obama did the opposite. Ignoring the Reagan model, or perhaps seeking to grab whatever power they could at the outset, Obama and the Democrats of 2009 appeared never to consider coalition building. To the contrary, Obama's lack of leadership was glaring for all to see on two main fronts: policy choices and their implementation.

On the policy front, Obama's first major act was the passage of the so-called "Stimulus Bill." Keeping in mind that there has never been a majority in the Country that has backed run-away spending, let alone the fact that Republicans lost control of Congress over spending in 2006, the sheer size of the Stimulus Bill at $787 billion quickly divided the House of Representatives and the Nation. Worse yet, Obama's first act was not to empower Americans to rise to the occasion, but like Johnson, he wanted to use government to level the playing field and to spread the wealth - a policy that is the sworn enemy of achievement.

On the policy execution front, Obama hardly fared better when it came putting together the details of the Stimulus Bill. Remembering that Obama had never managed a large enterprise before, let alone the largest enterprise in the World, Obama's troubles with the Stimulus Bill deepened because he left far too much of the responsibility related to that bill to Democrats in the Congress and Nancy Pelosi in particular.

Pelosi had spent the previous two years as Speaker of the House only to see most of her spending priorities languish under a Republican Senate and president. Freed of such restrictions, and all but taking the reins from Obama, Pelosi and friends jumped at the chance to be in power and reward their political friends with a massive spending bill that had far less to do with economics than pork barrel politics.

Republicans, on the other hand, knowing that they had lost in 2006, in part because they spent too much, lined up in unison against the Stimulus Bill much like the Republicans of 1993 who voted against the Clinton tax increase. In time, it would have the same effect. It would do so because the party-line vote for passage of the Stimulus Bill on February 17, 2009, less than one month into Obama's presidency, set the table for the Democrats to lose the House in the Fall of 2010.

But that divisive vote was not all from Democrats in the month of February of 2009. Just two days after the passage of the Stimulus Bill, President Obama announced the Homeowners Affordability and Stability Plan. It was an unprecedented $75 billion plan to help homeowners avoid foreclosures. Combined, those two Democrat initiatives would dramatically change politics in America.

Indeed, rather than view Obama's narrow victory the previous Fall for what it was, it was apparent that the 2009 Democrats believed that they had unchained license. They more than disregarded coalition building - they literally ignited a political firestorm rarely seen in American history. I am speaking, of course, of the *Tea Party Movement.*

While discontent had been growing for years among those **Silent No More**, including protests in New York and Seattle in February of 2009, its pent-up nature was still looking for a spark. That came in the form of Rick Santelli on February 19, 2009. It was on that day that this long-time reporter took to the airwaves on CNBC with what has become known as "the rant."

According to Santelli and with reference to the foreclosure program:

> "The government is promoting bad behavior...I'll tell you what, I have an idea. The new Administration's big on computers and technology. How about this, President and new Administration, why don't you put up a Web site to have people vote on the Internet as a referendum to see if we really want to subsidize the loser's mortgages, or would we like to at least buy cars and buy houses in foreclosure and give them to people who might have a chance to actually prosper down the road and reward people who actually carry the water instead of drink the water...This is America. How many of you people want to pay for your neighbors' mortgages that has an extra bathroom and can't pay their bills?"

The political answer to that question galvanized many of the varied voices across the American political spectrum and changed the political calculus of American politics. Before we get to that analysis, however, the 2009 Democrats were hardly finished picking fights with Americans.

Following that controversial policy with another, the Obama administration began to push Cap & Trade - a policy designed to warm the hearts of Global Warming, now Climate Change, enthusiasts. While it is unsurprising that those on the Left, who arrogantly think they can socially engineer the lives of free people, also think they can engineer the climate of a 4.7 billion year old planet - there is little doubt that pushing that major agenda was not a consensus building maneuver. The still growing economic troubles, matched with an electorate unquestionably divided on the issue even before Obama's election, meant that Obama did not ultimately get a legislative victory on the issue and his policy divided the Country even further. Obama would not take no for an answer, however, and in time used the unelected EPA to push his agenda – further alienating himself from portions of the electorate.

During the same time, Obama insisted on trying the mastermind of the 9/11 attacks, Khalid Sheikh Mohammed, in civilian courts, in of all places, New York City. It was a jarring ideological decision to treat KSM as a "criminal" versus the warring terrorist that he is. Even the average American could see that that decision could have had profound negative consequences for decades to come. Even more amazing was

Obama's decision to fight with New York over the place of the trial. It is a political fight he could not win regardless of the outcome of the trial. Obama compounded his troubles when he attempted to pass it off as the decision of his Attorney General and, in the end, they had to reverse the decision altogether. The reversal, however, did not change the fact that in 2009, this represented another fight picked with Americans.

The biggest fight was yet to come, however. Obama's next effort was to push a massive ideological takeover of 17% of the US economy in the form of a Health Care bill. Dubbed the Patient Protection and Affordable Care Act, the bill would prove to be one of the most controversial legislative acts in American History, and the most so since the passage of the Civil Rights Act in the 1960's.

The long and divisive process to passage for what would become known as ObamaCare began not long after the passage of the Stimulus Bill and the announcement of the $75 billion Homeowners Affordability and Stability Plan. In other words, Obama and the Democrats in Congress were on an unprecedented spending spree. The central character in all their plans was government - not **We the People**.

In the ensuing months, the Health Care bill would be debated at a fever pitch and often in less than gentile tones. The Democrats, rather than seeking consensus, openly derided the bill's opponents. Charges of racism and even treason were leveled against the bill's opponents.

Of course, the target of such charges was often the growing Tea Party Movement. According to pollster Scott Rasmussen, members of the diverse and decentralized movement "think federal spending, deficits and taxes are too high, and they think no one in Washington is listening to them, and that latter point is really, really important."

To Rasmussen's point, the Democrats were force-feeding Americans their Big Government programs despite vocal opposition within the Halls of Congress and without. Rather than heed such voices, the Democrats attempted to demonize the Tea Party Movement after initially down playing its very existence and, even more so, its political power. Indeed, Speaker Pelosi would say that it was an astro-turf movement rather than a true grass roots movement. Democrat Senate leader Harry Reid agreed and held up a piece of astro-turf at one point. Their disdain turned ugly in the hands of union members, who, in August of 2009, at a town hall held by a Democrat Congressman, beat up a Tea Party supporter just after handing out "Don't Tread on Me" flags.

The heavy-handed approach of the Democrats only fueled the fire of the Tea Party activists whose ranks grew in numbers and party affiliation throughout 2009 with increasing momentum. Still undeterred, on Christmas Eve, the Democrats pushed through ObamaCare on another party-line vote of 60 - 39. The missing vote, of course, was that of Ted Kennedy's. He had died on August 25th of that year. The special election to replace Kennedy was slated just over weeks after the Christmas Eve Senate vote on ObamaCare.

The Democrats' decision to force a vote so late in the year provided even more incentive for those opposed to Obama's policies and for those who felt that Congressional leaders did not care what many on Main Street were thinking or saying. Their outlet was to nationalize the January 19th special election in Massachusetts as a referendum on the ObamaCare Senate vote and Scott Brown became their overnight hero.

Few expected Brown or any Republican to be able to win the seat in the weeks after Kennedy's death. But in the age of the Internet and 24-hour cable news, activist anger around the Country saw Brown raise enough money and awareness to win a Senate seat held by Democrats for decades. More than that, it convinced Tea Party members, Republicans and Democrats that the Tea Party Movement was not to be ignored - and, ultimately, it laid the ground work for the Congressional losses suffered by the Democrats that Fall.

Initially, the Scott Brown election led many to believe that the Democrats would abandon the push to have the House pass ObamaCare. The Democrat ideologues in Congress, however, had different plans. They had waited far too long to let the possibility of government healthcare slip away - and so, in March the House passed it and the president promptly signed it - without the transparency the Democrats had promised.[101] Americans had ObamaCare whether they wanted it or not and the polling at the time certainly indicated they did not.

As of this writing, a strong majority still did not and their hopes rested on an unprecedented effort by the States that filed suits to block the implementation of ObamaCare on Constitutional grounds. So intense were those sentiments that the long lost doctrine of "nullification" surfaced. Under that doctrine, the individual states of the late 1700's and early 1800's decided for themselves whether the federal government had overstepped its bounds and literally nullified its acts. In doing so, states like South Carolina and Georgia gave the Country some of its first Constitutional crises. Today, Idaho appears willing to go down that path by passing a law against allowing the enforcement of ObamaCare. All of which highlights the intense division Obama's policies and management of the Country has fostered. Unquestionably, both led to the Democrats losses in the Fall of 2010. They also gave us the Tea Party Movement.

---

[101] Obama had promised that the Health Care debate would be broadcast on CSPAN among many promises Democrats made to have unprecedented openness under their rule.

The Tea Party Movement

If we recall that government spending was 7 to 8 times as large in 2010 as it was 45 years earlier, or that it doubled in the previous decade, we begin to understand the genesis of the ***Tea Party Movement***. Of course, growth in government is not just a question of benign spending. With each dollar spent or borrowed, not only is someone taxed to an ever greater degree, but government gains more power over its citizens who, over time, become more and more its *subjects*. With few exceptions, the last seven decades of American politics has left many Americans feeling rather more like the latter.

In the time since President Regan said "government is the problem," a growing chorus of the ***Silent No More*** came to believe, not incorrectly, that neither major political party was focused on our ***Freedom Lost*** - let alone the dangers of government spending out of control. The Nation's debt became a more prominent subject with a growing number of voters believing that the national debt will never be repaid. Historically, we know that Third Party movements emerge amidst such gaps between voters major and political parties. The ***Tea Party Movement***, in large part, is that story.

As 2009 unfolded, their rising sentiment played out in a 21st Century multi-media playing field. It gained ground faster than those movements of less technological ages and its prominence was perhaps best measured by its detractors.

In politics, there is an old adage that if they are not attacking you, you are irrelevant. If so, you may well be able to judge the relevancy of the *Tea Party Movement* by the amount of fire it drew in the 2010 election cycle. In mid-2009, the "Tea Party" was merely "astro-turf" in the eyes of those on the Left. By 2010, they were deemed more than extreme in the eyes of the Main Stream Media, the Democrats leadership and Left in general. But was that really the case?

Before we answer the question, keep in the mind the intensity of the attacks the Tea Party participants faced. They are referred to as "earth-shatteringly stupid"(Rolling Stone Oct. 14, 2010 edition), "racist," "hard-right," and, of course, "extreme" – the latter of which will produce over 2.7 million Google hits. It also was the recent subject of Obama's characterization of "the Republican Party as all but taken over by Tea Party extremists."

So how extreme were the Tea Party participants in the 2010 cycle? Let's take a look. Among the Tea Party Groups, one of the most prominent is the Tea Party Express. I attended a few of their rallies and found that they championed the following slogans at one time or another on the side of their tour bus:

- Stop Out of Control Spending!
- No Government Run Healthcare!
- Reduce the Size & Intrusiveness of Government!

- End the Bailouts!
- Stop Raising our Taxes!

Do those slogans represent extreme views? Let's see what a few people have to say about them.

On Out of Control Spending: "Ongoing deficits may severely and adversely affect expectations and confidence, which in turn can generate a self-reinforcing cycle among the underlying fiscal deficit, financial markets, and the real economy."

On Government Run Healthcare: "What can we do about this? Well, you and I can do a great deal. We can write to our Congressmen and our Senators. We can say right now that we want no further encroachment on these individual liberties and freedoms. And at the moment, the key issue is, we do not want socialized medicine."

On Reducing the Size and Intrusiveness of Government: In 2004, we had a presidential candidate call the Patriot Act "an assault on our basic rights."

On the Bail Out Bills: In 2008, one Senate candidate called the 2008 financial bailout bill a "sacrifice at the altar of financial mismanagement."

On Stop Raising our Taxes: "Nor should the argument seem strange that taxation may be so high as to defeat its object, and that, given sufficient time to gather the fruits, a reduction of taxation will run a better chance, than an increase, of balancing the budget."

I suspect most Tea Party supporters agree with some or all of those comments. The authors of those comments, however, in order: Democrat Treasury Secretary Robert Rubin on spending, then Democrat Ronald Reagan on Healthcare, Democrat presidential candidate John Kerry on the Patriot Act, then Senate candidate now Democrat Senator Al Franken on the bailout and liberal lion economist John Maynard Keynes on taxes being too high.

It is always worthy, in any discussion – especially political - to put things in context. The fact that all of those quotes came from either current or former Democrats – some rather liberal Democrats – should give you that context.

Today, an enormous number of voters, well exceeding 30% by some counts, support the Tea Party Movement. A majority of American voters want to repeal ObamaCare and cut taxes. Almost by definition therefore, the foregoing proves that the mantras of the Tea Party Movement, which have also included requests to respect the Constitution and having legislators read the bills on which they vote, cannot be considered extreme.

All of which leaves one conclusion, the demonization of the Tea Party is all that is left for a Democrat Party whose policies have failed and are out of touch with the American electorate.

Of course, on that point, John Kerry asserted that it was "out-of-touch" *voters* that were to blame for the Democrats woes. It is just that type of extreme arrogance that the Founders were against and, when coupled with bad policies, resulted in the changing of the guard in the Fall of 2010.

Before we return to our analysis of the 2010 elections, however, we should conclude our discussion of the effect of the Tea Party Movement in the 2010 cycle. First, perhaps the greatest effect of the Tea Party Movement, was and still is that legislators and members of Congress are once again asking the simple question when considering legislative action: Is this the proper role of government? The magnitude of that shift in axis of our national political discussion cannot be overestimated.

Second, no one could logically conclude that the Democrat losses would have been as high without the rise of the Tea Party Movement or that Republicans would have touted the Constitution and lower spending as much as they did. That is not to say that Republicans in that cycle would have gone along with Obama - after all, they voted in unison against the Stimulus Bill on February 17, 2009 before Rick Santelli even called for a Tea Party. It is to say, again, that the center of gravity of the political debate in the 2010 cycle was significantly moved toward the right axis and that contributed mightily to Democrat losses in the Fall of 2010.

As an overall perspective and as we look back on the results of the 2010 Fall elections, we can conclude that they were a simple referendum on the policies and tactics of the Democrats combined with worsening economic times. *There was no sense among Americans of Manifest Destiny - just diminished returns sponsored by government.*

Indeed, although Vice President Biden promised that unemployment would not rise above 8% as a result of the passage of the Stimulus, their reliance on government was ignored by the reality of economics. The Nation's unemployment rate pushed above 10% with the broader unemployment index reaching nearly 17% - a modern record was set for the number of months that unemployment was above 9%. Adding to voter misery, the Nation's foreclosure/mortgage crisis saw Americans lose $6 trillion in homeowner equity from 2006 to the end of 2010.

Putting all that together, the Democrats suffered those huge losses even without much effort by the Republicans. It was nearly a mirror image, magnified by the arrogance of Democrat leaders, of the dynamic that decided the 2006 and 2008 elections. The incumbent party once again was deemed to be the party of government - spending out of control and not reforming for the better in all three cases - and now there was a vigilant movement within American politics to make sure that those within government paid attention to the voices outside of government.

The only question in the wake of those three losses, was whether Republican leaders had taken to heart ***The Lessons We Should Have Learned***.

Chapter 11

The Lessons We Should Have Learned

**"I don't think much of a man who
is not wiser today than he was yesterday."
Abraham Lincoln**

It is, of course, presumptuous for anyone to sit in judgment on the collective wisdoms of millions of voters and attempt to bring order to their varied voices. Will and Ariel Durant, authors of **The Story of Civilization**, an eleven volume set, in their **Lessons of History**, asked writers of such ambition:

"Have you derived from history any illumination of our present condition, any guidance for our judgments and policies, any guards against the rebuffs of surprise or the vicissitudes of change?

Have you found such regularities in the sequence of past events that you can predict the future actions of mankind or the fate of states?

Is it possible that, after all, "history has no sense," that it teaches us nothing, and the immense past was only the weary rehearsal of the mistakes that the future is destined to make on a larger stage and scale?"

Comforted by the fact that the Durants proceeded to "compress a hundred centuries into a hundred pages of hazardous conclusions," it seems incumbent upon me to draw the few obvious conclusions from the past fifty years.

Lesson No. 1: Challenging America Matters

As we look back on the Presidencies of the last the last 50 years, most would agree that Kennedy's and Reagan's stand out as most dynamic and to this day the most iconic. The Presidencies of Eisenhower, Johnson, Nixon, Ford, Carter, and Bush 41 and 43 and Clinton simply do not wear as well. The reason lies in the fact that Kennedy and Reagan responded to difficult times by challenging America to reach new heights. Neither fell back on government to achieve their major domestic goals. In the face of difficult times, both sought to ignite the American Spirit through private initiatives. Cutting tax rates, dramatically, was their calling card. Not only did the economy respond to their policies, but by all accounts Americans did as well.

By contrast, the Presidencies of Eisenhower, Johnson, Nixon, Ford, Carter and Bush 41 and Clinton (and now Obama) are not marked by any great sense that the American people had a newfound self-respect or achieved unparalleled goals. No great challenge was laid down by them. Nor is it coincidental that all of them pushed policies that relied mostly on government, not individuals, in the face of difficult times. The presidency of Bush 43 started out as reformist and cut taxes, but Bush was not able to sustain those achievements. In the end, his domestic agenda slipped away.

The lesson here would seem manifest. The dulling limits of government constrain not only the hopes of its people but the potential success of their leaders. The way forward, even amidst difficult times, lies not with taxing one set of people to purportedly help another, but by fostering the conditions by which Americans can realize their dreams.

Lesson No. 2: Pro-Growth Tax Cuts Work, Politically and Economically

Lesson One, it seems, is the most important lesson of all and empirically, the easiest to prove. Nevertheless, it is surprising to see the number of Republican "leaders" who have yet to heed the lesson.

Lesson 2(A): Tax Cuts Work Politically

During the last 5 decades, only 3 presidents could be said to be true champions of pro-growth policies: Kennedy (whose policies were enacted by Johnson), Reagan and Bush 43. All three followed presidents that did not believe in such policies. All 3 achieved political realignments and/or political milestones – the other 6 presidents did not.

Kennedy. As we have seen, Kennedy's policies helped the Democrats obtain huge majorities in both Houses of Congress. In just ten years, the Democrats went from a Minority Party in Congress to huge majorities in both Houses: reaching highs of 68 – 32 seats in the Senate in the 1964 election and an astronomical lead of 295 seats to 140 seats in the House that same election.

The difference in policies between the Kennedy and Eisenhower administrations on the major issues of the day, including but not limited to the three Pillars of *The New Conservative Paradigm*, were not so great so as to cause such a political realignment – except on the issue of the economy, i.e. taxes. The hallmark of their differences was the Kennedy cuts versus the Eisenhower caution. The Kennedy majorities would take two decades to even begin to reverse in earnest – and by who? The next president to champion his policies: President Ronald Reagan.

Reagan. The center piece of the Reagan Revolution was most certainly pro-growth tax cuts. Beyond the economic benefits, they engendered the "No New Taxes Pledge" - a policy pledge that has basically defined presidential campaign politics ever since. Consider the following subsequent history:

- Reagan, the tax cutter, crushed Carter who allowed the tax burden to rise through bracket creep.

- Reagan wiped out Mondale who promised to raise taxes.

- Bush 41 defeated Dukakis, a life-long tax increaser, by promising "No New taxes."

- Clinton defeated Bush 41 by promising tax cuts in the face of Bush 41's tax increases.

- Clinton raised taxes dramatically and even more dramatically the Congressional Republicans, who all voted against the tax increase, took back Congress for the first time in 40 years.

- Clinton defeated Dole despite Clinton's tax increases because Dole (who was against the Kennedy cuts) was known for voting for tax increases and refused to take the No New Taxes Pledge - meanwhile, Clinton campaigned anew for tax cuts.

- Bush 43 campaigned for tax cuts and defeated Gore who characterized tax cuts as a "risky scheme," and

- Bush 43, the proven tax cutter, defeated John Kerry who promised to raise taxes and Bush achieved increases in his

Congressional majorities in 3 consecutive elections for the first time in many decades.

- Obama, promising 95% of Americans tax cuts defeated John McCain who was an unsteady voice for prosperity.

In other words, in 8 out of the last 8 presidential elections, the winning candidate promised tax cuts. In those same 8 elections, the candidate perceived as a tax increaser or at least unsteady on the subject, lost - except Clinton who lost the US Congress two years before but defeated Dole another tax increaser.

Again, the reason why tax cutters tend to win since Reagan's time (beyond good economic results) is that the American electorate views that issue as a question of whether the candidate favors the needs of individuals and families (tax cuts) or whether candidates favor the needs of government (tax increases). For tax cut advocates, it is the modern day equivalent of fighting city hall and it has enduring political power. For the presidents that follow through on their promise, it is a reflection of their basic point of view that *We the People* should be the agent for societal change.

That is why it is difficult to *hazard* any other conclusion from the foregoing except the following: If you want to win the presidency, campaign as a tax cutter. If you want to make a lasting political difference, champion large supply-side cuts. If you want to lose, the unquestioned route is to side with government and push for tax increases.

Why any Republican would suggest tax increases and thereby blur the lines between the parties - especially since *tax cuts raise revenue and tax increases over time do not* - in the face of such empirical evidence is difficult to fathom. Nothing need more be said and, any Republican leader who fails to understand the foregoing, nay - who fails to trumpet the foregoing - is doomed to repeat *History*'s mistakes.

While that may be the ultimate lesson for Republican leaders, it is up to every day Republicans, activists and voters alike, to discourage any candidate who thinks otherwise.

Lesson 2(B): Tax Cuts Work Economically

If it was still was an open question as to whether tax cuts can boost an economy prior to Reagan, there can be little doubt of that now. As we have seen, once the bad effects of Carter's stagflation were wrung out of the economy, the Nation's economy grew at a 3.8% growth rate from 1983 to 1989. Between 1974 and 1981, the growth rate had been just 2.8%.[102]

We also know that twice before Reagan, presidents gave American major marginal tax cuts and twice before the

---

[102] Supply Tax Cuts and the Truth About the Reagan Economic Record by William A. Niskanen and Stephen Moore, http://cato.org/pubs/pas/pa-261.html

American Economy boomed: Kennedy/Johnson (a cut in the marginal rate tax rate from 91% to 71% resulting in 5.8% growth in 1964, and by 6.4% percent in 1965 and 1966) and the Harding-Coolidge tax cut (a cut in the marginal rate tax rate from 71% to 24%) that resulted in the Roaring Twenties, i.e. the economy grew by 59 percent between 1921 and 1929.[103] Although doubters still persist on the Left, the fact that robust economy activity occurred each time major rate cuts occurred - with no other significant common feature - places the issue beyond rational questioning.

Beyond the growth rate, the Reagan years also settled the question as to whether lower tax rates result in higher tax revenue. Total tax revenues climbed by **99.4%** during the 1980s.[104] That followed a **62%** increase for Kennedy and **61%** increase during the 1920s.[105] These charts demonstrate the dramatic rise in tax revenues following those 3 major marginal rate tax cuts.[106] Seeing should amount to believing, especially for Republicans.

---

[103] "The Historical Lessons of Lower Tax Rates" by Daniel J. Mitchell, Ph.D. http://www.heritage.org/Research/Taxes/BG1086.cfm

[104] Same.

[105] Same.

[106] Charts from the Heritage Foundation.

The Reagan Years

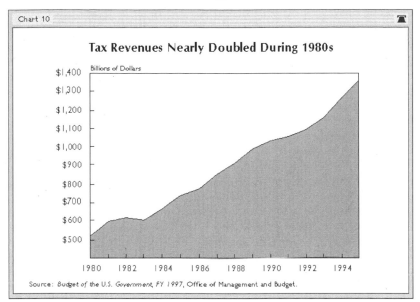

Chart 10

Tax Revenues Nearly Doubled During 1980s

Billions of Dollars

Source: *Budget of the U.S. Government, FY 1997*, Office of Management and Budget.

As for the Bush 43 cuts, beyond revenue growth in 2004 of 5%, the 15% in 2005 and similar rates in 2006 and 2007, consider the following:

> "In the six quarters after Bush's tax cuts, real GDP expanded at a 4.6 percent annual rate, much faster than the 2.5 percent pace of the six earlier recovery quarters. Consumer spending jumped from 2.8 percent to 3.9 percent.

> "Business investment in new plants and equipment surged to 13.4 percent from only 1 percent before the tax cuts. Personal income jumped to a 5 percent growth rate, nearly double the earlier speed of 2.6 percent.

The average employment gain (combining both surveys) was 2.4 million compared with virtually no gain before the tax cuts. Corporate profits, without which businesses cannot create jobs, now stand at a record $1.118 trillion - 56 percent above their recession trough, 25 percent above the prior recovery peak of the late '90s, and at a near-record 9.5 percent of GDP.

Broad stock market averages have jumped 60 percent from their lows. Home ownership is at an all-time high, as are existing home sales. U.S. household wealth stands at a record $51 trillion."[107]

As of July of 2007, tax revenues had increased $700 billion after the Bush tax cuts (the largest ever increase over a 3 year span) and even the *New York Times* was required to admit revenue gains following the tax cuts as opposed to tax increases. Although the June 13, 2005 *Times* article called the "sharp increase" "unexpected," for Republicans it should be anything but unexpected. The experiences of Coolidge, Kennedy, Reagan and Bush should once and for all settle the question: If you want to raise tax revenue, cut tax rates.

---

[107] "Barreling Ahead into 2005" by Larry Kudlow, National Review Online, http://www.nationalreview.com/kudlow/kudlow200412300923.asp

Lesson 2(C):

Over Time, Tax Hikes Do Not Work Economically

If *History* is clear that lower tax rates spur the economy resulting in higher tax revenues, it is also clear that the opposite occurs as well: If the government raises tax rates, in time, the government will receive less revenue over time than if they had not raised taxes at all. Recall the 14th Century quote that "It should be known that at the beginning of the dynasty, taxation yields a large revenue from small assessments. At the end of the dynasty, taxation yields a small revenue from large assessments."

Need proof?

- In 1930, President Herbert Hoover raised the marginal tax rate from 25% to 63%. Roosevelt pushed them to 79% that same decade. [108] Although those tax hikes were not the only cause of the Great Depression or its length, they certainly contributed a great deal to both.

- In 1991, Republican Governor Pete Wilson's 1991 increased tax rates in California in response to a budget

---

[108] "The Historical Lessons of Lower Tax Rates" by Daniel J. Mitchell, Ph.D. http://www.heritage.org/Research/Taxes/BG1086.cfm. Other contributing factors to the Great Depression included the Hawley-Smoot Tariff Act of 1930 that reduced trade and the federal government's decision to permit the money supply to shrink by nearly $1/3^{rd}$.

deficit. Years 2 and 3 of that increase resulted "in a revenue drop of $2 billion."[109]

- Income tax revenue grew slower under Clinton – and his tax hikes - than under Reagan and his tax cuts.[110] In other words, the Clinton tax hikes slowed the Reagan growth rates as did the Bush 41 hikes.

In a Picture Not Words

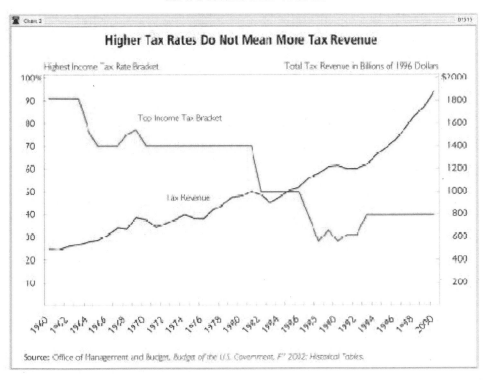

[109] "California's Tax Follies: States Can't Tax Their Way Back to Prosperity" by Lawrence J. McQuillan and Andrew M. Gloger, published in National Review Online, http://www.nationalreview.com/nrof_comment/comment-mcquillan040703.asp

[110]   Are   Supply-Siders   All   Washed   Up?   by   Stephen   Moore http://www.cato.org/dailys/6-06-97.html

Disciples of Clinton and Robert Ruben are wont to claim that tax hikes resulted in balanced budgets in the later Clinton years. It is empirically correct that there were balanced budgets during some of the Clinton years. The tax hikes, in the short run, did net more tax revenues, but just like overfishing harms a fish population, the Ruben/Clinton tax increases led to a recession starting in 2000.

However, that tax hike-induced recession *negated prior revenue gains*. The relevant question, therefore, is not - in the short run, can higher tax rates raise tax revenue, but over time, do they do so in the aggregate? The answer is no, because they curtail future economic growth and lead to recessions which lead to lower tax revenues.

Lesson 2(D): Tax Hikes Do Not Work Politically

At this point, it hardly seems debatable, but the fates of the Goldwater Republicans, the Mondale Democrats, the Dukakis Democrats, the Bush 41 Republicans, the Wilson California Republicans, and the Gore, Kerry and Daschle Democrats should be enough to convince even the most ardent - ***Make tax increases your program and it is likely to be your last.***

Lesson 2(E): The Name of the Game is Reform

We have seen that the Democrats cornered the market on voters in the '60s by offering tax cuts for the haves and social programs for the have nots. The modern day equivalent to such a strategy is offering tax cuts for the haves and government reform of underperforming programs for the have nots.

Voters of the Internet age have become savvy enough and educated enough to know that the answer to every problem is not more money or a larger government program. Republican and Democrat losses in the elections of 2006 and 2010, brought on by the big spending habits, are a testament to that. Voters' rejection of Big Government solutions is not only that they are paying enough taxes already, but also that they understand Big Government has become less responsive to their local needs. In effect, they have bought Reagan's argument that "government is not the solution to our problem. Government is the problem," or perhaps Clinton's suggestion that the era of Big Government is over.

As the complexities of our times grow, there is no reason to believe that *Reform* won't be the name of the game in health care, education, and so many other issues.

Lesson Number 3:

Big Political Gains Occur When Leaders Promote *The Three Pillars* and Inspire Their Country to Achieve Greatness

Only three of the last ten presidents had significant success and lasting effect on their party's stature in Congress: Kennedy, Reagan & Bush 43 (pre-2006). All three had essentially the same program: Cut taxes, be strong on defense, believe in your Country and its place and mission in the World and be respectful of its traditions - the three Pillars of *The New Conservative Paradigm*. Nixon, Clinton and Obama proved you can win without all three but Kennedy, Reagan and Bush 43 proved that championing all three can change the tide.

Kennedy, Reagan and Bush also engaged voters in a higher purpose. Kennedy asked his Countrymen to help achieve:

> "the kind of peace that makes life on earth worth living, the kind that enables men and nations to grow and to hope and to build a better life for their children -- not merely peace for Americans but peace for all men and women -- not merely peace in our time, but peace in all time."

Reagan believed that because "no arsenal, or no weapon in the arsenals of the World, is so formidable as the will and moral courage of free men and women" there would be a "march of freedom and democracy" that would change the World.

For his part, Bush 43 cemented his place in *History*, during his second Inaugural Speech in 2005, when he inspired so many as he told the World that:

> "There is only one force of history that can break the reign of hatred and resentment, and expose the pretensions of tyrants, and reward the hopes of the decent and tolerant, and that is the force of human freedom.
>
> We are led, by events and common sense, to one conclusion: the survival of liberty in our land increasingly depends on the success of liberty in other lands.
>
> The best hope for peace in our world is the expansion of freedom in all the world."

In reading those words from Kennedy, Reagan and Bush 43, ask yourself how far their inspirations are from Lincoln:

> "In *giving* freedom to the *slave,* we *assure* freedom to the *free*—honorable alike in what we give, and what we preserve. We shall nobly save, or meanly lose, the last best, hope of earth."

or Washington:

> "As Mankind becomes more liberal, they will be more apt to allow that all those who conduct themselves as worthy members of the community are equally entitled to the protections of civil government. *I hope ever to*

see America among the foremost nations of justice and liberality."

It is a lesson of our time, if not all times, that great leaders inspire their fellow citizens to achieve goals that transcend their times and their present day hardships.

In heeding that lesson, Kennedy produced huge majorities for the Democrats. Reagan changed presidential politics and began the realignment which President Bush 43 enjoyed into 2005 by being the first president to win Congressional increases in three straight elections.

The power of **Pillar Number Two**, however, should not be overestimated. History has shown that, in the last forty years, the incumbent party does not fare well if they are prosecuting sustained foreign wars. Recall that the Vietnam War fell to Democrat Lyndon Johnson. Republicans suffered the ill effects of the Iraq War in the 2006 Midterm elections – especially since they had no counter-balancing record of achievement – and in the 2008 presidential election, although to a lesser degree. Political parties, therefore, should be wary of starting prolonged wars in favor of using overwhelming force and being able to secure the resultant peace. If they are caught in a long war, they best provide reform at home so that voters have an alternative storyline to follow other than the distortions of the Media.

Lesson Number 4: Trash Your Country,
Its Ideals or Its Defense at Your Peril

As we have seen, during the late 1960s, the Democrats were in some disarray. They were just four years removed from the huge 1964 Congressional victories. The Kennedy/Johnson tax cuts had produced unprecedented growth. Yet they managed to lose the 1968 election. Why? In part because Johnson was not the pro-growth advocate that Kennedy was. However, it was not as if the Republicans stole the issue from the Democrats. To the contrary, the Republicans were vocally against the Kennedy cuts. The Republicans' 1968 presidential candidate, Richard Nixon, did not repudiate those objections and certainly did not offer a tax cutting program of his own. Indeed, one year later he would raise tax rates on capital gains – an anti-growth measure. Thus, tax policy was not the determining factor of the 1968 election.

What changed, of course, was the view of America by the leaders of the Democrats. Their infighting over the Vietnam War left their party with a distinctly anti-American message which lost out to Nixon's Silent Majority. Thus, it can fairly be said, if the tax issue is neutralized by muddled voices, i.e. read the voices of Johnson, Nixon and Humphrey, Pillars Two and Three may be determinative.

The Democrats' skepticism towards America and its Purpose was a weakness carried over into the Carter years. It was instrumental in causing the loss of American prestige around the World as was demonstrated dramatically by the Iran hostage crisis. The Reagan victory was due, in part, to his rejection of such timidness which helped overcome the negative Media coverage of the Reagan tax cut proposals.

The rise of the effectiveness of the Christian Right, the Bible Belt and the Red States that so dominated the electoral map also presented strong evidence that modern voters value the party that respects their values.

Even so, the Clinton years may well demonstrate the lesser role of Pillars Two and Three to Pillar Number One, pro-growth policies. We have already concluded that Bush 41 lost the 1992 election because he abandoned his No New Tax Pledge and Clinton was promising tax cuts. Clinton won that election even though the Dems were still behind on Pillars 2 and 3 – although, it could be argued, that Clinton benefited from his Baptist ties in taking some Southern States from the less vocally spiritual Bush 41. By in large, however, the Dems as a whole had not changed the dynamic.

Clinton won reelection despite raising taxes and despite the fact that Republicans stayed ahead on Pillars Two and Three and Clinton's high-profile troubles. Why? Because Bob Dole was not a credible surrogate on **Pillar Number One**, tax cuts. His was a muddled voice much more in the mold of Johnson,

Nixon, Ford and Carter – none of whom had economic legacies. As a result, Dole was not able to convince the Country that he, a proven tax hiker, should replace another tax hiker, Clinton.[111] That factor was not helped by the fact that Dole did not come out for tax cuts until $^2/_3$ of the way into the campaign.

In sum, for purposes of our discussion, it remains evident that if the parties are indistinguishable on the issue of taxes, depending on the circumstances, being behind on Pillars Two and Three can cost you a presidential election, i.e. 1968, but it may not, i.e. 1996. It should be noted, however, that since 1996, the divide on Pillar Number Three has deepened and it may play a more determinative role in the future if Independents react adversely to ever more aggressive policies of the Left.

---

[111] It also did not help that Dole simply was not a man of obvious faith. As a result, Dole did not inspire the so-called Evangelical Vote.

A Review of the Effect of Three Pillars
In Modern Presidential History
(Incumbent party on the left hand side for all charts)

The 1960 & 1964 National Elections

Pillars	Nixon (1960)	Kennedy		Johnson (1964)	Goldwater
No. 1 Pro-Growth		x		x	
No. 2 Defense	x	x		x	
No. 3 Family/ Traditions	x	x		x	x
Winner		Kennedy		Johnson	

The 1960 election featured the sitting Vice President Richard Nixon against JFK. The difference between the Eisenhower administration and the Kennedy administration on foreign policy and traditional values was not dramatic. The difference in the election was the difficulty in electing sitting vice presidents, in general, and specifically in the wake of the three recessions the Nation endured under Eisenhower. Once in office, Kennedy challenged Americans to achieve more and gave them the tools to do it by promoting pro-growth policies leaving the Republicans behind on the tax issue and on the defense issue through effectively branding Goldwater as potentially reckless in the 1964 election. The Republicans lost both national elections and suffered politically in Congress for years after.

The 1968 & 1972 National Elections

Pillars	Humphrey (1960)	Nixon		Nixon (1972)	McGovern
No. 1 Pro-Growth					
No. 2 Defense		x		x	
No. 3 Family/ Traditions		x		x	
Winner		Nixon		Nixon	

In the 1968 and 1972 elections, neither party espoused pro-growth policies. Bother were promoters of government. The Democrats, however, to their misfortune, turned vocally against America, its defense and its traditions. The anti-war, anti-traditional values party lost both elections under those circumstances. However, in the absence of a leader on **Pillar Number One**, there was no political re-alignment in Congress or otherwise.

1976 National Election

Pillars	Ford (1960)	Carter
No. 1 Pro-Growth		
No. 2 Defense	X	
No. 3 Family/ Traditions		x
Winner		Carter

The 1976 election was decided, of course, under the shadow of Watergate. It was also decided in an era where neither party was particularly distinguishable domestically except that the Republicans were against the tax and spending excesses of the Democrat Congress but not against tax and spending. As such, the Republicans were the "Me Too" Party on promoting government, taxes and spending and they had lost their lead on the family/tradition issue because of the scandals of the Nixon administration and the perceived decency of Carter and his Baptist ties.

Ford nearly recovered from his decision to pardon Nixon to catch Carter at the end. But without an economic program, and in the relative calm of foreign affairs, the election was in all likelihood decided by something other than one of the three Pillars. It was decided in the aftermath of Watergate which produced a variant of **Pillar Number Three**. Certainly, no realignment there either.

1980 & 1984 National Elections

Pillars	Carter (1980)	Reagan	Reagan (1984)	Mondale
No. 1 Pro-Growth		x	x	
No. 2 Defense		X	x	
No. 3 Family/ Traditions		X	x	
Winner		Reagan	Reagan	

The 1980 and 1984 elections featured the first election since 1964 in which a party held a strong position on all three Pillars. The result? Reagan Democrats, the political realignment of voters and the beginning of a political realignment in Congress.

1988 & 1992 National Elections

Pillars	Bush (1988)	Dukakis	Bush (1992)	Clinton
No. 1 Pro-Growth	?		No	?
No. 2 Defense	x		x	
No. 3 Family/ Traditions	x		x	x
Winner	Bush			Clinton

The 1988 election featured the first victory by a sitting vice president since Martin Van Buren in 1836 – pure proof of the enduring Reagan re-alignment. Bush campaigned *promising* no new taxes. Fortunately for the elder Bush, who once used the phrase "voodoo economics" to describe Reagan's pro-growth policies, he ran against a weak Democrat opponent on all issues in 1988. He would not be so lucky the second time around in 1992.

As we have seen, Bill Clinton was not about to repeat the mistakes of Carter, Mondale or Dukakis. Even though the elder Bush continued the Republicans' run on Pillars Two and Three, Clinton capitalized on Bush's default on **Pillar Number One**. Clinton campaigned for tax cuts and won despite trailing on **Pillar Number Two**. Southern Baptist ties minimized any Republican advantage on **Pillar Number Three**. In retrospect, the 1992 election is enduring evidence of the prominence voters place on **Pillar Number One**. In other words, or to paraphrase Clinton's advisor James Carville, it's the pro-growth policies stupid.

1996 National Election

Pillars	Clinton (1996)	Dole
No. 1 Pro-Growth		
No. 2 Defense		x
No. 3 Family/ Traditions		
Winner	Clinton	

The 1996 election should have been a no-brainer for Republicans. Clinton had forfeited the lead on the tax issue and the Republicans had taken back Congress. Nevertheless, this election appears to defy the charts and the Pillars.

The explanation lies in the fact that Clinton had the power of the incumbency, raised huge amounts of money and had the help of the ever more influential Major Media. The Republicans had the weakness of incumbency – that is not a reference to the presidency. No, it was a reference to the fact that in the 1996 election the Republicans nominated their next in line – even though there was nothing compelling about his candidacy.

Far from compelling, Dole was a government insider and known tax hiker who refused to take the No New Tax Pledge. Also, Dole was not comfortable discussing the value of morality or religion. As such, he failed to motivate Republicans and values voters. The Democrats, meanwhile, mercilessly defined Dole prior to Dole receiving matching funds in the late summer.

One can only wonder the fate of the 1996 election if the next in-line for Republicans had been Jack Kemp.

2000 & 2004 Presidential Elections

Pillars	Gore (2000)	Bush		Bush (2004)	Kerry
No. 1 Pro-Growth		x		x	
No. 2 Defense		x		x	
No. 3 Family/ Traditions		x		x	
Winner		Bush		Bush	

The 2000 and 2004 elections were similar to the 1980 and 1984 Reagan elections. The Republicans, perhaps learning from the Bush 41 debacle and the Clinton/Dole loss, nominated a pro-growth candidate who talked about individual achievement and proceeded to win two elections in a row. Bettering that, they won three consecutive national elections when you consider their Congressional gains in 2002.

2008 Presidential Election

Pillars	McCain	Obama
No. 1 Pro-Growth		x
No. 2 Defense		
No. 3 Family/ Traditions		
Winner		Obama

The 2008 election was decided on the economy. It was so bad, and the Media so harsh by the end of 8 years of President Bush, that it would have been hard for any Republican to win. But as you look at the chart above, the fact remains that the Republicans in 2008 did not champion any of the Three Pillars. McCain simply and painfully for Republicans was not a pro-growth voice – to the contrary, he championed a huge government program in the form of a mortgage bailout. The length of the ongoing wars in Iraq and Afghanistan neutralized Obama's foreign policy weaknesses and wound up motivating the Left more than the Right. That is why no advantage on **Pillar No. 2** is given to either side. McCain's muted voice on family and respect for America's traditions left him without that advantage as well.

Have You Noticed the Critical Lesson?

As you look back, through the charts, there is one critical lesson to be gained. There is not a single election in which a presidential candidate lost when that candidate was *convincingly* ahead on the issue of taxes, i.e. who was for the individual and families, versus the champion of government – not one. That is perhaps the enduring lesson of *The New Conservative Paradigm*.

Chapter 12

Lessons in Action

**"Insanity: doing the same thing over and over again
and expecting different results."
Albert Einstein**

If Einstein is right, and there are few grounds on which to dispute his point, then presumably an equally true corollary would be Political Insanity: *refusing to do what works*. Perhaps the other side of that coin is the saying that "Those who do not learn from history are doomed to repeat it."[112] The simple question for the Republican Party, in the coming decade, will be whether it relies on what worked in the past or whether

---

[112] First said by Spanish born American philosopher George Santayana (1863 – 1952) and repeated by President Harry Truman.

it will voluntarily walk away from the lead it has by ignoring the past.

As we have seen, the decade of 2010 and beyond will present an enormous fiscal challenge for our Country. If the Republican Party is to build on its Majority Party status in the House, it will have to renew a critical aspect of the Reagan Revolution or risk minority status.

As we think ahead, however, we would do well to remember the historical dynamic that governments do not start out *large and efficient* and wind up *small and inefficient*. Quite to the contrary, the *History* of governments, including our own, is that they start out small and decentralized and relatively responsive to the governed. Since power abhors a vacuum and therefore loves to centralize, governments tend to grow and grow until they reach the point of being more large and inefficient than actually helping the governed.

Indeed, our own colonies needed to be coaxed into being a Nation. In reaction to their experience with the British Monarchy, the Colonists drafted a decentralized Articles of Confederation. They were agreed to by Congress on November 15, 1777 (after 16 months of debate) but not ratified and in force until March 1, 1781 - nearly three and one half years later. Not centralizing enough to hold the Nation together or protect it, they were then replaced in 1789 by the ratification of the Constitution – all told, a 12 year process. Centralization, however, did not stop there.

Perhaps the easiest way to understand the centralization dynamic is through the lens of the federal budget. In 1821, the federal budget was but $15 million dollars. One hundred years later, just before the Great Depression, the federal government expenditures were $2.92 billion – and then, we were off to the races:[113]

1925	2.92 billion
1930	3.32
1935	6.4
1940	9.47
1945	92.71 (WWII)
1950	42.56
1955	68.44
1960	92.19
1965	188.23
1970	195.65
1975	332.33
1980	590.95
1985	946.39
1990	1,252.53 trillion
1995	1,519.13
2000	1,788.83
2005	2,399.8
2006	2,660
2007	2,730
2008	2,900
2009	3,107
2010	3,552
2011	3,820

---

[113] All figures are gross dollar amounts not adjusted for inflation.

The chart starts just before the Great Depression because it is a good point of reference for what lies ahead. Prior to the Great Depression, there were no New Deals and the federal government was comparatively small. In response to the serious crisis, a crisis badly exacerbated by government, the societal reaction was not to fall back on days of self-reliance or even to blame government - but, instead, to look for an even larger governmental solution to the problem – a pattern familiar to all of *History*. With that, the federal government began a process of swift growth that continues to accelerate.

The growth in the last 25 years alone is stunning. In the 1970s, in gross terms, spending tripled. It tripled again by 1995 and has nearly doubled since then. Today, the federal government spends over $20 of every $100 spent each day. By 2075, if we stay on our current path, the federal government will spend at least $40 out of every $100. Long before 2075, however, the US will be confronted with a challenge which could be larger than the Great Depression.

The Triple Witching Decade

In stock trading, the Triple Witching hour occurs four times a year when stock options, stock-index options, and stock-index futures all simultaneously expire. Markets can often be *volatile* during that hour as investors cash out. In 2007, I wrote that "For the US, the Triple Witching decade will be 2010 to 2020 –

if not before. If we are not careful, our investors may well cash out." Today's reader knows that that moment has arrived.

We are in the throes of Triple Witching Decade because:

1. The US Public/Private Pension Crisis is upon us
2. Social Security is all but under water
3. The Medicare Crisis (state and federal) is not far behind

The breadth of this book is certainly not sufficient to cover those coming crises, but a short reflection is required to place the magnitude of those issues in context.

The US' Private Pension Crisis

According to the federal Pension Benefit Guarantee Corporation (PBGC), the government agency charged with guaranteeing pension benefits for some 44 million employees of *private* sector companies that fail, as of 2005, "defined benefit pension plans in the US have promised $450 billion more in benefits than they have in assets."[114]

---

[114] "Are Pensions the Next Fiscal Crisis?" by David C. John, Tim Kane, Ph.D., and Rea S. Hederman, Jr., The Heritage Foundation, WebMemo #756, June 2005,
http://www.heritage.org/Research/SocialSecurity/wm756.cfm

In 2007, I noted that: "a new Government Accountability Office (GAO) report that details the level of underfunding in the 100 largest defined benefit pension plans . . . shows that underfunding is getting worse."[115]   Indeed, at one point in 2004, at least 14 companies that comprise the S&P 500 owe their workers more in pension payments than what the whole company would be worth in liquidation.[116]

By November of 2009, the Pension Benefit Guarantee Corporation reported that "its potential exposure to future pension losses from financially weak companies" had tripled from fiscal year 2008 to 2009.[117]   Such problems result in the Pension Benefit Guarantee Corporation perennially landing on the Government Accounting Office's "high risk" watch list.

At this time, the US taxpayer does not pay for the bailouts of such unfunded pensions. Annual per employee premiums pay for the "insurance."   However, if a severe shortfall in the program occurred, "a taxpayer bailout of the agency is inevitable."[118]   It may well be inevitable because the history of

---

[115] Ibid.

[116] http://www.forbes.com/personalfinance/estate_planning/2004/08/12/cz_b c_0812pensions.html

[117] http://www.reuters.com/article/2009/11/14/us-financial-pensions-idUSTRE5AD01Q20091114

[118] "Are Pensions the Next Fiscal Crisis?" by David C. John, Tim Kane, Ph.D., and Rea S. Hederman, Jr., The Heritage Foundation, WebMemo #756, June 2005, http://www.heritage.org/Research/SocialSecurity/wm756.cfm

our Country, at least since the 1930s, is that in times of economic crisis, the "solution" is ever larger government. Witness the Savings & Loan bailout during the late 1980s and early 1990s which cost taxpayers somewhere over $150 billion dollars.[119] It is no stretch to assume that may happen again, with respect to the private pension crisis, and only the most naïve would believe that the pressure on Congress for such action would be anything less than monumental. The private pension crisis, however, is just the tip of the iceberg.

The Public Pension/Medicare/Social Security Crisis

As bad as the private pension crisis is and will continue to be, the existing Pension/Medicare/Social Security crisis will dwarf the private pension crisis. Today, Social Security, Medicare and Medicaid amount to 40% of the federal budget. That is expected to rise to 60% by 2021 and consume all tax revenue by 2025.[120] The simple truth, however, is that we don't have the money to pay for those programs.

---

[119] "The Cost of the Savings and Loan Crisis: Truth and Consequences" by Timothy Curry and Lynn Shibut, http://www.fdic.gov/bank/analytical/banking/2000dec/brv13n2_2.pdf

[120] "Democrats Throw 'Ice Cold Water' on Social Security Revamp" by Heidi Przybyla, Bloomberg, February 25, 2011

In 2007, I provided my readers the following quote that described the extent of the crisis:

> "long-term economic health of the United States is threatened by $53 trillion in government debts and liabilities that start to come due in four years when baby boomers begin to retire. . . . The $53 trillion is what federal, state and local governments need immediately — stashed away, earning interest, beyond the $3 trillion in taxes collected last year — to repay debts and honor future benefits promised under Medicare, Social Security and government pensions. And like an unpaid credit card balance accumulating interest, the problem grows by more than $1 trillion every year that action to pay down the debt is delayed."[121]

The effects of the recession that dominated the 2008 election cycle, and continues to this writing, only made those predictions worse.

In 2007, it was projected that Social Security would start taking in less than it pays out in 2017. The projection made by the Congressional Budget Office in early 2011, however, was that Social Security system will run a $45 billion deficit for 2011. By some measures, since the 1980s the Social Security system has collected over $2.5 trillion more than it had paid out. In practice, politicians used that so-called Social Security

---

[121] "The Looming National Benefit Crisis" by Dennis Cauchon and John Waggoner, USA TODAY, http://www.usatoday.com/news/nation/2004-10-03-debt-cover_x.htm

surplus to bail out their other expenditures. Now, Congress will have to use general fund dollars to bail out Social Security. In 2007, I wrote that: "By 2020, the combined Medicare/Social Security deficit will exceed $200 billion per year." Now the Congressional Budget Office projects that "Excluding interest, surpluses for Social Security become deficits of $45 billion in 2011 and $547 billion over the 2012–2021 period." If that is not enough to scare you, "Overall, over the next 75 years, Social Security faces a $7 trillion unfunded liability . . ."[122]

As for Medicare, the numbers are much worse. The current projection of Medicare unfunded liability, over those same 75 years, is a staggering 5 times as much as the Social Security deficit - $36 trillion – or over 9 times our current budget.

Can federal spending really continue to grow that fast without a total collapse of the system? Keep in mind that federal spending jumped over 8.5% in 2005 under a Republican Congress and a Republican president and that the "new Medicare prescription drug benefit, [enacted under a Republican Congress and a Republican president] increased the government's unfunded obligations by $8.1 trillion over the next 75 years." [123]

---

[122] "Democrats Throw 'Ice Cold Water' on Social Security Revamp" by Heidi Przybyla, Bloomberg, February 25, 2011
[123] "Time for the Federal Budget Process to Include Unfunded Entitlement Obligations" by Alison Acosta Fraser, The Heritage Foundation, http://www.heritage.org/Research/Budget/bg1818.cfm

Worse yet, "there is no budgetary consideration of the actual financial commitments resulting from policy changes enacted by Congress because they are paid well into the future."[124] In other words, Congress spends with barely any consideration for future costs – all that matters is the budget for the current year. Want to enact a new spending entitlement? No problem, we have the money now. The future be damned.

State & Local Government Pension Crises

The problems of health care and public pensions, however, are not confined to the federal government. In California, a widely cited report from the Little Hoover Commission, in February of 2011, stated that the state's "Pension costs will crush government." California has an incredible 85 public pension plans. The unfunded liabilities for just the 20 largest of those plans, according to the Little Hoover Commission, exceeded $240 billion in 2010 – or nearly 3 times the state annual revenues. It was ¼ of that in 2007.

---

[124] Ibid.

Why Something Needs to Be Done

As I wrote in 2007, the point of this chapter is not to be an alarmist – although alarms should have gone off by now, if not well before now. The point is to have the reader understand that the next ten years could present the US with a challenge no less in size than the Great Depression or World War II. Unless we act as a Nation to get government under control, we are headed for a fiscal meltdown. That meltdown would result in a significantly lower standard of living for all Americans.

Of course, it is likely that the leaders of the Left will be of little help in this crisis. They will claim that the Republicans are abandoning the poor by advocating reduced government. In other words, they will demagogue these issues endlessly.

It should be obvious though, that we do a much larger disservice to those on the government dole by failing to address these issues now and thereby courting a future meltdown that could leave the poor with little to no services and no savings on which to fall back. Beyond that, the likely economic breakdown will leave them without jobs as well. Thus, to not get government under control will amount to abandoning the poor, not the opposite. Put another way, a bankrupt government is not a compassionate government.

So, what to do? Simply stated, we must act now and not wait for the storm to come ashore. As we consider what action to take, it must be noted that, contrary to Thoreau's admonition that "things don't change, we change," ***things have changed and** so have we*.

Things changed in that government has already grown out of control. Prior to World War II and the Great Depression, our federal government was still relatively small. It had room to grow. Now however, we don't have the option of 60 years of new, explosive, government growth. In that same time, we have changed. Most are tired of growth in government and endless taxes – many are ***Silent No More.***

All of which begs the question, that since the federal government spends over $20 of every $100 spent each day, does anyone really think Americans will stand idly by as we march toward 2075 when the federal government will spend at least $40 out of every $100?   Will Americans accept payroll taxes of 25%, such as in France, in addition to ever higher income and sales tax rates, to pay for these programs? Could we even reach such a point? Sadly, the answer is yes. But...it is not inevitable.

A Menu of Needed Reforms

At all times we need to remember that government is a man-made institution. It is an **un**natural disaster waiting to happen when it grows to such proportions. Quite frankly, Ronald Reagan would say in the face of the current spending crisis that:

> "The crisis we face is not the result of any failure of the American spirit; it is failure of our leaders to establish rational *goals* and give our people something to order their lives by."

As far as inevitability, Reagan said and would say again:

> **"I do not believe in a fate that will fall on us no matter what we do. I do believe in a fate that will fall on us if we do nothing."**

Thus, we can fairly conclude that doing nothing is not an option. We need to get about the business of establishing rational goals to reigning in the unsustainable growth in government before it hurts nearly everyone and helps a diminishing few.

One last dose of reality, however, as we start this process. Sadly, and obviously, we cannot always or even often count on the leaders of either party to do the right thing by controlling spending. It is an unfortunate truism that once elected, politicians, who otherwise knew government must be controlled, too often become overwhelmed by ***Edifice Complex*** – a psychological affliction that seems to require them to justify their political existence (1) by appropriating ever greater amounts of money to government programs, and/or (2) by having something built, i.e. a bridge, a building, etc., to which they can claim credit.

President Calvin Coolidge alluded to this affliction years ago when he stated:

> "Nothing is easier than spending the public money. It does not appear to belong to anybody. The temptation is overwhelming to bestow it on somebody."

Given the magnitude of pork barreling, by both Democrats and Republicans, over the many years since Coolidge made that remark (when the federal budget was under $3 billion – today it is $3 trillion), it seems logical to conclude that there is no known cure for the ***Edifice Complex***.

In the absence of that cure, quite frankly, it will be up to the ***Silent No More*** to lead our leaders out of this crisis. In other words, ***We the People*** must undertake a series of measures to reduce the opportunities for politicians to act out their spending urges.

The following is a list of reforms by which ***We the People*** can undertake to do just that. The list is not meant to be exhaustive, nor is the list an attack on any individual program. Instead, they are measures designed to (a) reform the programs we already have, and (b) change the structural components of modern government that permit the unsustainable, unlimited growth we face today.

In doing so, those reforms will not hurt the poor as the leaders of the Left will claim. They are common sense attempts to stop politicians from forcing our government over the edge and hurting the poor even more.

1. **Enact True Part-Time Legislatures**. There is no immutable law of physics which requires full-time legislatures. They are the favorite of politicians - not average Americans. Worse yet, full time legislatures violate President James Madison's desire for a citizen legislature that would retire to their normal jobs so as to reflect the common values of our citizens instead of the professional class our legislators have become. Furthermore, every day any legislature is in business is another day spending goes up not to mention tax rates and fees.

A part-time legislature reduces those temptations by as much as half. So, if you want to slow down spending, simply stated, give politicians less opportunity to do so, i.e. less days to tax and spend. Therefore, state legislatures should only be in session for four to five months out of the year. If they fail to pass a budget within that time, then the budget should revert to the expenditures of the prior year and the legislators pay should be reduced for failing to do their job.

2. **Enact Two Year Budget Cycles**. Simply stated, the federal and state governments should be required to budget two years at a time (such as Texas does), not the one year cycle most use now. That set-up offers the added benefit of requiring longer term planning. More importantly, two year budget cycles have a similar effect to that of a part time legislature. They reduce the opportunity of legislators to spend money in half again because, barring a super majority vote for a state crisis or a special session on a particular issue, budget items would be considered only once every two years. Combined with a part-time legislature, politicians would only have 4 to 5 months every two years to tax and spend compared to the 18 months most take advantage of now.

3. **Enact Real Budget Spending Limits**. Government growth, at least at the state level, should be restricted roughly to the growth in population and the CPI increase. Without budget real caps, legislators from all parties legislate with blank checks and credit cards with no limits. We must take away those blank checks and cancel those credit cards. In their stead, we should enact real budget caps. Colorado had an effective statute and

no surprise; it was one of the few states that did not have a fiscal crisis as a result of the Clinton-9/11 recession.

4. Require Accrual Based Government Accounting.

Quite frankly, the reason politicians spend without regard to the future is because there is no real consideration of future spending. Why? Well, in part, because government uses the "Cash Basis" method of accounting. "Cash-basis budgeting does not recognize the true costs of operating the federal government . . . Accrual accounting [on the other hand] is widely recognized as providing information that is superior to cash-basis recordkeeping and is used in business precisely because it forces [its users] to recognize and plan for future obligations."[125] In other words, each spending program would require its true long term cost to be carried on the federal books (unlike now), i.e. there would be long term planning and accounting. Since cash basis accounting does not – it has to go. Once voters see how poorly their politicians have managed their future, they may think twice about voting for incumbents that are irresponsible.

---

[125] "Time for the Federal Budget Process to Include Unfunded Entitlement Obligations" by Alison Acosta Fraser, The Heritage Foundation, http://www.heritage.org/Research/Budget/bg1818.cfm

5. **Require Cost-Benefit Analyses for all Programs**. Most government programs are enacted without a cost-benefit analysis. In other words, programs are enacted without a serious review of whether they will actually work. Moreover, funding for programs goes on and on without a rational determination as to whether the program is helping the needy – or whether the needy still exist for the program in question. Periodic cost-benefit Analyses of programs can lead to realistic determination of whether future programs make sense and whether existing programs should be modified to help their intended beneficiaries or whether they are still needed. That can result in better government and the reduction of wasteful spending.

6. **Require Zero Based Funding**. Most governments determine next year's budget by adding on to last year's budget. Rarely is an analysis considered or done of whether the prior funding met its goals, i.e. helping the needy. Further, given the mandates tied to most funding, i.e. restrictions as to exactly where money can be spent, wasteful funding can go on and on without real oversight. Requiring zero based funding will force legislators to review how your money is spent every year and will require them to justify each program – which takes time and reduces their ability to create new programs. That too can lead to better government.

7. **Sunset Government Programs**. Most government programs are enacted and never end – regardless of whether they are helping their intended beneficiary in the manner that was originally contemplated. If programs were sun-setted, i.e. terminated at a future date certain, before that date arrives, needed programs could be addressed with an eye to the problem as it exists at the time they are reconsidered - not as it did years before. In that way, outdated programs and taxes could be phased out in favor of other priorities like Medicare.

8. **Governments Must Move to Defined *Contribution* Programs and Away from Defined *Benefit* Programs**. It is the wont of politicians to guarantee an outcome to government pension beneficiaries. Unfortunately, "defined benefit" pension programs, as they are known, guarantee retirees a fixed amount each year such as their last year's salary. That results in massive unfunded liabilities for government pensions and social services because it has the effect of keeping retirees on the payroll for life. "Under the switch [to defined contribution programs], employees and employers (the government) would both contribute to an individual investment account. Upon retirement, the size of each public employee's pension would depend on the contributions made (including the employer match) and the personalized investment strategy the employee

used. This way, the state could still offer attractive retirement plans but lawmakers couldn't make promises they can't pay for."[126]

9. **<u>Government Employee Pension Benefit Increases Should Require Voter Approval</u>**. Any pension benefit must be voted on by taxpayers. You are paying the freight and therefore you should directly vote on whether there should be an increase in government pensions. Politicians have proven that they cannot be trusted with this issue. San Francisco County voters have this power and San Francisco programs are fully funded. That is so because in order get any pension increase, proponents have to demonstrate a balanced budget to the voters. Meanwhile, neighboring Contra Costa County, which does not send such increases to the voters, has a $2.5 billion funding deficit.

10. **<u>Outsourcing Non-Essential Services</u>**. The simple truth is that we cannot afford to pay for all of the government programs that are already on the books. Therefore, the question becomes: Do we care more about services being provided or who provides those services? Obviously, the answer is the

---

[126] "How to Keep Pension Promises on the Road to Solvency" by George Passantino http://www.rppi.org/pensionpromises.shtml

former, and therefore government at all levels must stop looking to be the provider of all services associated with government. For instance, it is not essential for government to be in the janitorial business. By doing so, however, the burden on taxpayers is higher because government must foot the bill for the retirement of all those employees as well as other costs associated with being an employer. Those costs, and countless others like them, could be reduced by outsourcing non-essential services thereby freeing up money in favor of other priorities like Medicare.

Those are just a few ideas for helping to bring governments back from the brink of bankruptcy. All of those *Reforms* can be enacted by ***We the People*** through the initiative process. In states such as Colorado, California and others, reform movements utilizing the initiative process are already underway – sometimes without the support of politicians. The remainder of the Country needs to join their revolution and place our so-called leaders on notice that spending without consequences will in fact have consequences for them.

A Game Plan for Republicans

The coming crises will not only challenge our Nation, but also test whether the Republican Party can be the Majority Party in Congress. Whether it will be the Majority Party will depend, of course, on whether it deserves that status.

As the coming spending crisis unfolds, the following "givens" must be kept in mind:

- It is more than likely that the Democrat leaders will simply demand new taxes and higher spending.

- The Party of *No* is historically the Minority Party.

- Therefore, as pensions, Medicare, Social Security and other large government programs reach critical funding junctures in the years just ahead, Republicans cannot simply say *No* – No to programs and No to voters. Nor can they campaign simply by saying we need budget cuts - lest they become the Party of *No* versus the party of handouts – the Democrats.

So the dilemma for the Republican Party is how to stay the Party of *Yes* during a budgetary crisis when spending must be reduced from the projected levels. The answer is by doing what works: (1) Stay firm on tax cuts because they produce greater revenues over time and (2) embrace true *Reforms*.

Beyond lower taxes, the "Yes" Republicans must provide real *Reform* designed to maximize taxpayers' resources not bureaucracies coffers. Reagan began the modern era of *Reform* from the moment he was elected. It was successful. Given the problems ahead, it would be insanity not to follow his lead.

By championing the *Reform* movement, the Republican Party will be offering the average voter something positive: better government and lower taxes. The Democrats, for their part, will fight reform at every turn and as a result: (a) will be the party of the status quo, i.e. Big Government, and (b) the **Party of NO** – no to *Reform*. Thus, the dynamic is in place for the Republicans to successfully champion the issue of *Reform* and thereby be the Majority Party nationally.

The Power of Yes

Keep in mind that one of the great successes of President Reagan was his ability to change the national mood. He was optimistic and America became so. Psychology 101 will teach you that people respond to positive images, actions and especially leadership. Positive agendas and positive leadership leads to majority status because, when it comes to voting, generally, voters like to vote *for* something more than they like to vote *against* something.

Therefore, the game plan for the Republican Party is simple: give them something to vote for and keep the Democrats on the defensive. Year after year, the Republican

Party and its leaders, state and federal, should put forth combinations of reform initiatives and legislative agendas driven by reforms.   In that way, Republicans can not only control the agenda – but give voters a reason to vote for them.

It is a winning, positive formula that should be replicated around the Country again and again.   Given that 2012 is just around the corner, and the fiscal crises are here, we cannot wait any more.   Republicans should act now, seize the higher ground and control the agenda of tomorrow.   In doing so, it can stay the Majority Party nationally.

Chapter 13

Final Thoughts & Hopes

**"Visualize this thing that you want, see it,
feel it, believe in it.
Make your mental blue print, and begin to build."
Robert Collier**

We have nearly reached the end of our journey. Along the way, we have heard from the great leaders in American History: Washington, Lincoln, Kennedy & Reagan to name a few.   Not surprisingly, they share an ability to inspire, but not just inspire. Each summoned their fellow citizens to *Higher Purposes*. Under each of them, Americans achieved more than could be anticipated under difficult circumstances. Certainly, that is one definition of leadership.

Amidst our review of history, we have discovered that our government is growing out of control with spending that has more than doubled in the previous ten years. We wonder whether any one person can govern this Country or some of its states. We have also learned, however, that we are not speaking just about 2007 or 2010. Indeed, the same held true for 1980. Spending rose dramatically in the 1970s at a time when the Cold War dragged on seemingly without an end in sight. Pundits wondered whether the presidency could be managed by just one person.

At the time, a leader came along – a true leader. His words are worth reading again:

> "We're not, as some would have us believe, doomed to an inevitable decline. I do not believe in a fate that will fall on us no matter what we do. I do believe in a fate that will fall on us if we do nothing."

Amidst such uncertainty, he suggested that:

> "The crisis we face is not the result of any failure of the American spirit; it is failure of our leaders to establish rational *goals* and give our people something to order their lives by."

The issues Ronald Reagan faced in the early 1980s are not much different than the issues we face today. Back then, neither the Democrat leaders nor government had answers to the malaise fostered by Jimmy Carter and the policies of our government during the preceding years.

Reagan had those answers and for a time he changed the course of government – choosing to rely on individual initiative - not government programs.   He was well aware that the government-made problems of inflation, slow growth and rising taxes were robbing Americans not just of their wealth but of their spirit as well.   So, in the face of government growth that was out of control, he willed the Congress to reduce spending.   He recognized that government was not the solution to our problems but, instead, that government was the problem - and so he set about reforming government through regulatory reform.   And, of course, he cut taxes because doing so was the economic equivalent of setting people free.

Those rational goals can serve our Nation once again. Within the next few years, along with the explosive growth of government, we will face a growing pension crisis, a growing immigration problem and a government that has no answers to the everyday problems of everyday Americans.

Quite frankly, the current crop of Democrat leaders seem to have no answers to those problems because their twin mantra of raising taxes and ever larger spending are no longer viable answers for a Country that is overtaxed and treasuries that are overdrawn.   The answer is *Reform* and the Republican Party can be and must be its champion.

We can take comfort in knowing that the path upon which we must walk is well worn with the Wisdom of Reagan. We should understand that the issues facing America call for answers that Republicans have and the Democrat leaders don't. And so, with Reagan's example in mind, Republican leaders have the opportunity to reject inevitable decline and they have the opportunity to set rational goals.

Those goals must once again affirm the Three Pillars of *The New Conservative Paradigm*. Our presidential and Congressional candidates and leaders must once again adopt a powerful agenda that preserves our freedom and simultaneously lifts our spirits. They cannot simply believe in the economic effects of tax cuts. They must passionately understand the nexus between tax cuts, freedom, inspiration and hope.

They must also understand that we are not interested in electing managers of our government. We want leaders that will change the course of government. Beyond that understanding they need to communicate that passion to the American people and let them know once and for all that they understand that they represent *We the People* - not government.

As grassroots activists, we must demand no less from our leaders and we must remind them at every turn that tax cuts and *Reform* led the way to the Republican majority in Congress – not spending, not tax increases.

The task we set out to achieve this time may well be difficult. Surely though, we cannot believe that the task we face compares with the task Lincoln faced on the morning of his inauguration as a president facing Civil War. It was Lincoln's principles and his resolve that led the way.

Lincoln's **Optimism** was essential as well and as we have seen, it is a trait shared by all great leaders. So we too must have that optimism and we must know that civilizations, like individuals, must always be looking ahead. We cannot "think of today's failures, but of the success that may come tomorrow."[127]

If we do, we shall be able to carry on the legacy of Ronald Reagan and we shall have it in our power to "begin again."

---

[127] Helen Keller

Acknowledgements

We are, in many respects, who we were – as a person, as families and even civilizations. In that light, I must thank all those family members, friends, teachers who helped weave the fabric of my life. They have brought me to today . . .

Chief among them are my parents. During the time I wrote the first edition of this book, my Mother fell quite ill with cancer and overcame it as she has previously. Since then, her health remains of deep concern. She unquestionably is the strongest person I have ever known. Every day she lives her life for her beliefs. This book is a small effort to honor her courage and her life . . . Incredibly, my Father fell ill with the same type of cancer as this book neared its original publication and now shares the disease that saw Reagan into the twilight of his life. Along with my Mother, he taught me that honesty, intellectual and otherwise, is more important than success. This book tells the truths as I now know them and with the skills that his strength and honesty have forged.

My parents also blessed me with seven brothers and sisters – all of whom have kept me on my toes through the years. We certainly all don't agree on the issues, but their intellectual vibrancy certainly nurtures mine. My sister Nicole deserves to special mention for her help with researching the original book and her work as an Editor of Politicalvanguard.com.

Since the original publication, I want to especially thank

~ CA State Senator Tony Strickland for helping me throughout my political career especially in becoming the Chairman of the California Republican Party.

~ Brian Sussman of KSFO for standing by me and providing me so much encouragement and help;

~ Joel Angeles for his friendship and hard work on my campaign;

~ Felicia Tweedy whose tireless volunteer work for my campaigns and the CRP has made it possible for to extend my efforts and communicate my ideas around the state;

~ Caroline Graham for helping so very much on this Second Edition and her constant help with my campaigns;

~ Ivy Allen for the incredible work editing the 2nd Edition.

From the original publication, I wish to thank the following for their kindness and encouragement:

~ Bruce and Valerie Schooley for some time encouraged me to write the original book and so here it is! They have supported my political endeavors at every turn including helping me with this book. I can't thank them enough.

~ Stephen Frank has been a great supporter of mine as well. He spent many an hour reading the early transcripts of this book as well as my many other writings as well as helping me become a State Party Chairman. Thanks again for all of your help.

~ Darcy Linn, thanks for all the work you have done not only for Politicalvanguard.com but also in reading the early transcripts of this book. Neither would have been possible without your help.

~ Gretchen Medel, thank you for all the work you do to making my political endeavors easier including reading the early transcripts of this book.

~ Greg Poulos – who has a Masters in US History – thanks for reading this book so closely and making sure the trees and the forest were kept in proper perspective.

~ Patricia Welch – thanks so very much for your help on my CRP work without which I could not spend the hours needed on this book.

~ Melanie Morgan who helped me at the very beginning to have my voice be heard.

~ Inga Barks of KMJ, Mark Carbonaro of KION, Mark Larson of KCBQ and Eric Hogue of KTKZ, all of whom have been so very kind enough to let my voice be heard.

To the many volunteers around the state of California who continue to fight for the Reagan Revolution every day and who have shown many me so many kindnesses including the volunteers of the Republican Party of Contra Costa, the California Republican Party and my many friends in the California Federation of Republican Women.

Finally, to my daughter Juliana from whom I learn from everyday and whose love keeps me going.